LIONEL MESSI

THE GREATEST PLAYER IN HISTORY

LIONEL MESSI
The Greatest Player in History

PREAMBLE

In the realm of football, where legends are born and records are shattered, there emerges a name that echoes through the ages, a name that transcends the boundaries of the sport itself. Lionel Messi, a prodigious talent hailing from the streets of Rosario, Argentina, has etched his name in the annals of history as the epitome of greatness. This book, penned by the esteemed author Jean Bercy, delves deep into the extraordinary journey of Lionel Messi, unravelling the threads of his unparalleled career and illuminating the essence of his genius. From the humble beginnings of a young boy with a dream, to the pinnacle of success as the greatest player to have graced the game, Messi's story is one of sheer determination, unwavering passion, and unmatched skill. With meticulous research and profound admiration, Bercy paints a vivid portrait of this footballing maestro, capturing the moments that defined his legacy and the indomitable spirit that propelled him to greatness. As we embark on this captivating exploration, we invite you to witness the extraordinary rise of Lionel Messi, to marvel at his artistry, and to join us in celebrating the unrivalled legacy of the greatest player in the history of football.

TABLE OF CONTENTS

INTRODUCTION 3
CHILDHOOD YEARS OF MESSI 7
THE INCREDIBLE RISE OF MESSI 19
THE IMPRESSIVE SKILLS OF MESSI 37
MESSI'S DEEP UNDERSTANDING OF THE GAME 43
THE ASTONISHING ABILITIES OF MESSI 52
EXPLORING MESSI's ROLE AS A STRIKER 59
MESSI'S ROLE AS A PLAYMAKER 65
MESSI'S SCORERING PROWESS 69
MESSI DRIBBLING PROWESS 76
MAGNIFICENT MESSI'S FREE KICK 79
MESSI No. 10 82
MESSI AND FC BARCELONA 85
MESSI AND ARGENTINA 97
LET THE STATS SPEAK 102
MESSI: THE UNMATCHED PHENOMENON 107
HEAD-TO-HEAD: MESSI VERSUS PELÉ 114
HEAD-TO-HEAD: MESSI VERSUS MARADONA 122
THE BATTLE OF MESSI AND RONALDO 129
THE GAME REINVENTED BY MESSI 153
MESSI, BEST PLAYER OF ALL TIMES 157
THE 2022 WORLD CUP RECITAL 162
INSIGHTFUL QUOTES FROM MESSI 173
WORLD QUOTES ABOUT MESSI 184
CONCLUSION 189
REFERENCES 191

INTRODUCTION

Lionel Messi, undeniably a football legend, has not only captivated the hearts of countless fans but has also become a role model whose influence extends far beyond the pitch. Renowned football commentators, with their vast knowledge and expertise, unanimously hail Messi as an exceptional player who has left an indelible mark on the sport. Moreover, his unparalleled skills and unwavering dedication have prompted numerous admirers to emulate his style, both on and off the field.

Football, a game that encompasses a multitude of intricacies such as tricks, tactics, strength, and strategic thinking, has undergone a remarkable transformation throughout the years. What was once merely an enjoyable pastime has evolved into a morality play, a source of valuable life lessons that people eagerly absorb. The sport has transcended its recreational roots, becoming a powerful medium through which individuals learn about teamwork, perseverance, and the pursuit of excellence.

Nevertheless, at its core, football remains a game fueled by passion. It is this fervor that ignites the hearts of both players and spectators alike, creating an atmosphere that is unparalleled in any other sport. When contemplating the essence of this passion, it is impossible not to evoke the name of Lionel Messi. His extraordinary talent, combined with an unwavering love for the game, has forever etched his name in the annals of football history. Whenever commentators or fans reflect upon the profound impact that football has on their lives, Messi's name is invariably invoked, symbolizing the unparalleled inspiration and devotion that the sport elicits.

Drawing on these compelling ideas, this essay delves into the captivating life of Lionel Messi, meticulously examining his extraordinary accomplishments as a football player, while shedding light on the remarkable records he has established. It is imperative to recognize that the inception of football society is intricately intertwined with class consciousness, an undeniable reality that manifests itself in our everyday existence, where we frequently bear witness to players exhibiting unparalleled brilliance on the field.

There is no denying the fact that this essay focuses solely on the most significant records achieved by Messi. It is a universally acknowledged truth that records are bound to be surpassed, however, breaking certain records is an immensely challenging feat, even for an exceptionally talented player. Nevertheless, Messi has managed to shatter an astonishing number of records, and this essay meticulously highlights and pays tribute to this remarkable accomplishment.

This essay passionately and resolutely advocates for the belief that tough individuals are capable of enduring and overcoming challenging circumstances. By examining Messi's lifestyle as a prime example of an environment characterized by exceptional and long-lasting brilliance, alongside a culture of tolerance, dedication, and unwavering determination, it becomes evident why he has become a role model for both his peers as a world-class football player and future generations as a trailblazer. It is no surprise that Messi stands alone as the sole athlete to have been honoured with eight FIFA Ballon d'Or awards and European Golden Shoe awards, solidifying his unparalleled success and undeniable influence in the world of sports.

CHILHOOD YEARS OF MESSI

Lionel Messi, one of the greatest football players of all time, entered this world on June 24th, 1987, in the vibrant city of Rosario, located in the Santa Fe Province of Argentina. His proud parents, Jorge Messi and Celia Cuccintini, brought him into a family rich in cultural diversity. Lionel's paternal lineage boasted a blend of Italian and Spanish roots, with ancestors who had migrated from Marche and Catalonia to Italy. On the other hand, his mother and her kin were of pure Italian descent.

In addition to his parents, Lionel shared his childhood with three beloved siblings who were his constant companions. His older brothers, Rodrigo and Matias, stood by his side, guiding and motivating him, while his younger sister, the delightful Maria Sol, brought joy and warmth to their lives. Despite their modest means, the Messi family thrived on a deep passion for sports, particularly football, which bound them together. They poured their hearts into the game, dedicating countless hours to watching, coaching, and playing it.

Lionel's father, Jorge, toiled diligently in a steel factory, working hard to provide for his family, while his mother, Cecilia, contributed to their livelihood by taking on part-time domestic work. The demands of their jobs sometimes meant that Lionel and his siblings had to fend for themselves, as their parents were absent. Yet, despite these challenges, the Messi family remained unyielding in their love and support for one another.

From an early age, Lionel's extraordinary talent on the football pitch began to shine. His family recognized his potential and nurtured his skills, ensuring he had every opportunity to excel. This unwavering dedication to their son's sporting aspirations became a cornerstone of their lives, shaping their collective identity and fueling their dreams.

In the face of adversity, the Messi family found solace and unity in the world of football. It became a powerful force that connected them, providing them with solace and happiness. Through their shared love for the game, they transcended their circumstances, proving that true wealth lies not in material possessions, but in the bonds of love and the pursuit of a common passion.

From a young age, Lionel Messi displayed an unwavering passion for sports, particularly football. Alongside his brothers Rodrigo and Matias, as well as his cousins Maximiliano and Emanuel Biancucchi, who would also go on to become professional football players, Messi immersed himself in the game. The seeds of his talent were sown at the tender age of five when he joined the Grandoli, a local club where his father served as coach.

However, it was his maternal grandmother, Celia, who truly ignited Messi's early drive as a player. Celia, a constant presence at his training sessions and matches, provided unwavering support and encouragement. Tragically, her passing just before Messi's eleventh birthday left an indelible mark on him, deeply affecting his young heart.

In the face of this profound loss, Messi turned to his faith as a source of solace and strength. A devout Catholic, he found solace in his spiritual beliefs and began to pay tribute to his beloved grandmother in a unique way. Every time he scores a goal, Messi looks up to the heavens, pointing to the sky as a heartfelt homage to Celia.

This simple gesture not only honors the memory of his grandmother but also serves as a constant reminder of the profound impact she had on his life and his journey as a footballer. Through his unwavering dedication, Messi continues to carry the spirit of Celia with him on and off the field, forever grateful for her role in shaping him into the iconic athlete he has become.

According to official records, Lionel Messi began his football journey at the tender age of six, joining the renowned club Newell's Old Boys. Under the guidance of his coach, Adrian Coria, Messi's talent blossomed. During his remarkable six-year tenure at Newell's, he astoundingly scored close to 500 goals, leaving spectators in awe of his incredible abilities. Adding to the excitement, his team delighted crowds during halftime by showcasing mesmerizing ball tricks.

The undeniable brilliance displayed by Messi during this period has led many to argue that his greatness had already surfaced. This sentiment is supported by the fact that his team suffered only a single defeat in four years, a testament to his immense impact on the field. However, it is more plausible to believe that Messi's exceptional football skills were gradually honed, as he dedicated himself to constant improvement even before reaching the age of ten.

Messi's early years at Newell's Old Boys laid the foundation for his extraordinary career, setting him on a path to become one of the greatest footballers the world has ever seen.

Undoubtedly, Messi's initial foray into the world of football was marked by an exceptionally gifted and passionate team known as "The Machine 87." Their extraordinary talent and unwavering love for the game left an indelible mark on the hearts and minds of all who witnessed their brilliance. However, fate dealt a cruel blow when Messi, at the tender age of eleven, was diagnosed with a growth hormone deficiency originating from complications in his pituitary gland. This condition, characterized by an inadequate production of growth hormone, posed a formidable obstacle to his physical development, and hindered the natural process of cell reproduction and growth.

During that period, the monthly expense for growth hormone treatment amounted to no less than $1000. Unfortunately, Messi's father's health insurance policy could only cover the cost for a limited period of two years. While Newell, the club Messi was associated with at the time, initially pledged to assist with the treatment expenses, they ultimately reneged on their promise. As fate would have it, when Buenos Aires of the River Plate discovered Messi's exceptional talent, they too assured him of their support for the growth hormone treatment. Tragically, the economic downturn in Argentina rendered the club unable to fulfill their commitment, leaving Messi and his family burdened with the financial strain of his crucial medical needs.

Despite possessing immense talent, Messi encountered his first significant obstacle. Despite the sympathy expressed by his local clubs, none of them were able to provide the necessary assistance. It was not due to any malicious intent on their part, but rather the result of their financial constraints. Regrettably, they were unable to bear the cost of his treatment.

Amidst the numerous challenges that Lionel Messi faced, a sudden twist of fate came his way with the arrival of Charles "Charley" Rexach, the Sporting Director of FC Barcelona. Recognizing Messi's potential, Rexach extended a helping hand by offering to cover his medical expenses, but with a condition - that Messi would eventually make the move to Spain. This proposition posed a difficult decision for Messi and his family, who found themselves at a crucial crossroad, with multiple paths to choose from. With limited alternatives, they reluctantly accepted Rexach's offer.

In September 2000, when Messi was just 13 years old, the family orchestrated a try-out with Barcelona. While

Charley Rexach was eager to sign him, the board of directors at Barcelona expressed hesitancy towards this unconventional move. It was highly unusual for European clubs to recruit foreign players at such a tender age. However, on December 14th, 2000, the Messi family took a bold step and issued an ultimatum to Barcelona, demanding tangible proof of their commitment. In this pivotal moment, Charley Rexach rose to the occasion, demonstrating his unwavering faith in Lionel Messi's abilities and offering him a contract.

In February 2001, Lionel Messi and his family made the life-altering decision to relocate to Barcelona, settling into an apartment near the revered FC Barcelona stadium, Camp Nou. This marked the beginning of Messi's journey with the club that would eventually propel him to unparalleled heights in the world of football.

During Messi's initial year in Spain, his involvement with the infantile team was limited due to a transfer conflict with his former club, Newell, as well as the restrictions placed on him as a foreign player. Consequently, he could only participate in friendly matches and the Catalan league. With minimal playing opportunities, Messi faced the challenge of familiarizing himself with FC Barcelona's strategies and style of play. Already somewhat introverted prior to his move, the atmosphere within his new club further isolated him, with his teammates treating him as if he were unable to communicate. As time went on, he experienced homesickness when his mother, brothers, and little sister relocated to Rosario, Italy, while he remained in Barcelona with his father.

After spending an entire year honing his skills at the prestigious Barcelona youth academy, La Masia, Lionel Messi's talent and dedication finally earned him a coveted spot in the Spanish Football Federation in 2002. This marked the beginning of his journey into the world of professional football, where he would showcase his exceptional abilities and forge lifelong friendships with fellow prodigies like Cesc Fabregas and Gerard Pique.

At the tender age of 14, Messi successfully completed his growth hormone treatment, a crucial milestone in his development. This propelled him to become an integral part of Cadets A, Barcelona's renowned "Baby Dream Team," known for their unwavering determination and unmatched skill on the field. With Messi's exceptional talent and unwavering commitment, he quickly emerged as a key player, leaving spectators awestruck with his mesmerizing dribbling, lightning-fast pace, and remarkable goal-scoring abilities.

In the remarkable 2002/2003 season, Lionel Messi made his mark as a rising star in the world of football. Playing for Cadets A, he showcased his exceptional talent by scoring a staggering 36 goals in just 30 games, setting a new record for the highest number of goals. Not only did he dominate the field with his scoring prowess, but he also led his team, Cadets A, to an unprecedented triple crown victory, triumphing in the league as well as both the Spanish and Catalan cups.

However, amidst his remarkable achievements, Messi faced a challenging moment in his early career when he suffered a broken cheekbone during a crucial league match. Despite the injury, Messi's determination and resilience shone through as he defied the odds. Although he was required to wear a protective plastic facemask to start the game, he fearlessly removed it and proceeded to score two incredible goals in just ten minutes before being substituted. This display of sheer skill and bravery left spectators in awe and further solidified Messi's reputation as a true football prodigy.

As the 2002/2003 season drew to a close, Lionel Messi's exceptional performances caught the attention of renowned British club, Arsenal, who extended an offer to him. This marked Messi's first opportunity to join a club outside of Spain, an enticing prospect for any young player. However, displaying unwavering loyalty and commitment to his current team, Barcelona FC, Messi made the bold decision to remain in Spain. In contrast, his friends and fellow footballers, Fabregas and Pique, opted to pursue their careers in England.

Messi's choice to stay with Barcelona FC not only demonstrated his strong bond with the club but also hinted at the immense potential he saw in his future with the Spanish giants. This decision would prove to be a pivotal moment in his career, as it set the stage for the countless achievements and accolades that would follow.

The current stage of Messi's professional journey has the potential to reshape the beliefs of those who previously believed that his life solely exemplified resilience, perseverance, hard work, and determination. Today, numerous fans can effortlessly envision the truth behind Messi's remarkable success story: he propelled himself towards becoming the greatest professional footballer, even in the face of daunting circumstances that encircled him. By delving into the earlier section of this essay, countless readers will wholeheartedly embrace the idea that Messi's beginnings were indeed arduous, yet he triumphed over immense adversities and hurdles.

THE INCREDIBLE RISE OF MESSI

Lionel Messi possesses an extraordinary ability to orchestrate plays, making him an exceptional playmaker on the field. His presence alone instils a sense of caution in opposing teams, as they are fully aware of the formidable "Messi factor." Time and time again, Messi surpasses expectations, leaving spectators in awe as he effortlessly accumulates goals and assists, ultimately securing victory for his team. When Messi is at the pinnacle of his performance, even the most formidable competitors are left in his wake. It is no wonder that players, commentators, and fans alike regard him as the unrivalled leader among his peers.

Messi's impact on professional football will undoubtedly be etched in the annals of history, as his immense contribution to the sport transcended borders, leaving an indelible mark both in Italy and at his cherished club, Barcelona. However, it is essential to recognize that this contribution did not manifest overnight; rather, it unfolded gradually, underscoring the universal truth that change is an ever-present force in our lives. Inarguably, Messi's career stands as a shining testament to the perpetual evolution that defines him. From his early days to his meteoric rise, he has exemplified a remarkable ability to adapt and transform, showcasing a relentless pursuit of excellence that has become his trademark. In every match, every season, and every milestone, Messi's unwavering commitment to growth and evolution has propelled him to unprecedented heights, solidifying his status as an icon of the beautiful game.

Playing for the junior system ranks in 2000 was the catalyst for Messi's extraordinary career. It was crystal clear that he was destined for greatness as he swiftly rose to become the most prominent footballer in the world, mesmerizing audiences while representing five different teams. His exceptional talent was evident from a young age, as he walked away with the player of the tournament award in four international preseason competitions with the Juveniles B.

Although he only played one official match with the Juveniles B, Messi's incredible skills caught the attention of the Juveniles A team, where he made an immediate impact by scoring an impressive 18 goals in just 11 league games. Remarkably, at the tender age of 16, Messi was already a game-changer, using his formidable abilities to rejuvenate a struggling Juveniles A first team during the international break. But his rise to stardom didn't stop there.

With his relentless brilliance on the field, Messi soared from the bottom to the top. He swiftly ascended through the ranks of the junior system, leaving a trail of awe-inspiring performances in his wake. It was no surprise when he finally made his league debut on October 16, 2004, against RCD Espanyol. At such a young age, Messi had already become a force to be reckoned with, leaving spectators in awe of his incredible talent.

On a fateful day etched in Messi's memory forever, he experienced an overwhelming surge of joy and excitement. Engaging in rigorous training sessions with both Barcelona A and B teams, Messi's exceptional skills caught the attention of none other than Ronaldinho, the superstar of Barcelona at the time. Astonished by Messi's remarkable performance during a practice session, Ronaldinho boldly proclaimed that Messi possessed the potential to surpass even his own greatness. This declaration not only forged a deep bond between the two players but also led to Ronaldinho affectionately referring to Messi as his "little brother."

It is crucial to highlight that Messi's momentous breakthrough arrived the following year on May 1, 2005, against Albacete, when he scored his first goal for Barcelona. This remarkable achievement was made possible by an assist from none other than Ronaldinho himself. Notably, this goal added another feather to the cap of the 17-year-old Messi, as he became the youngest player in La Liga history to find the back of the net, a record that was later surpassed by Bojan.

After successfully acquiring Spanish citizenship in September 2005, Lionel Messi embarked on his highly anticipated debut in the prestigious Champions League. The stage was set against the formidable Italian club, Udinese, where Messi, initially introduced as a substitute, unleashed a mesmerizing display of skill and finesse. Teaming up with the legendary Ronaldinho, the duo's on-field chemistry was nothing short of magical, captivating the hearts of fans worldwide. The spectators were so enthralled that they couldn't help but compare Messi and Ronaldinho to extraordinary identical twins, as their seamless coordination and unrivalled dexterity left everyone in awe. While it may sound like an exaggeration, the fans' enthusiasm only reflected the undeniable brilliance exhibited by these two extraordinary talents.

Messi's exceptional skills in the Champions League were undeniable, as he confidently scored an impressive six goals in just 17 appearances. This remarkable feat only served to solidify his already outstanding reputation as a player of immense talent.

It was on Messi's birthday, June 24, back in 2005, when he took a significant step forward in his career. Signing his first contract as a senior team player with Barcelona, he embarked on a journey that would see him hold this coveted position until 2010. From the very beginning, Messi's impact was undeniable, as he immediately proved himself as a starter with sensational performances that left fans in awe.

One match against Fabio Capello's Juventus showcased Messi's brilliance. His display on the pitch was so extraordinary that it earned him high praise and commendation at the iconic Camp Nou stadium. This exceptional showing caught the attention of Capello himself, who was so impressed that he was willing to loan Messi to other clubs, with Inter Milan even expressing interest in buying his contract from Barcelona.

However, Messi's loyalty and dedication to Barcelona were unwavering. Despite tempting offers from other clubs, he chose to remain with the Catalan giants. This decision was met with great joy and relief from Barcelona fans, who were overjoyed to see their beloved player commit his future to the team. In recognition of his unwavering loyalty, Messi's contract was extended for the second time in just three months, ensuring his presence on the team until 2014.

Messi's journey was one marked by exceptional talent, unwavering loyalty, and a relentless pursuit of greatness. His achievements in the Champions League and his unwavering commitment to Barcelona only served to enhance his reputation as one of the greatest players of his generation.

However, fate dealt Lionel Messi an unforeseen blow. Just as the age-old saying suggests, life's journey is not always smooth sailing; it can serve as a magnifying glass for both elation and anguish. This proved to be the case for the renowned footballer. A devastating muscle tear in his right thigh eventually forced him to depart prematurely from the illustrious Champions League. Despite his relentless efforts to regain his physical prowess in time for the grand final on May 17th, 2006, the heart-wrenching news arrived – he was deemed unfit to partake in the crucial match. Overwhelmed by profound disappointment, Messi's spirit was so shattered that he refrained from joining in the jubilant celebrations alongside his Barcelona comrades, who had triumphantly clinched the titles of Spain and Europe.

As the 2006-2007 season unfolded, Lionel Messi's rise to prominence was undeniable. No longer a substitute, his exceptional performances on the field earned him a permanent spot in the starting eleven. With each match, Messi's brilliance shone through, leaving spectators and commentators in awe. In 26 appearances, he found the back of the net an impressive fourteen times, showcasing his unrivaled talent.

Such was his impact that pundits began to proclaim Messi as the standout player of the starting squad, surpassing even the first ten players. His skills and abilities seemed to transcend those around him, elevating his status to unprecedented heights. Football records started to crumble under his influence, with one remarkable feat being his hat trick against arch-rivals Real Madrid in the iconic El Clasico match.

Not only did Messi achieve this remarkable accomplishment, but he also made history as the youngest player in twelve years to do so. With each goal he scored, he kept his team in the game, equalizing the score after every Real Madrid strike. The match was an intense battle that extended into overtime, ultimately ending in a thrilling 3-3 draw. Messi's impact on that game was undeniable, solidifying his status as a game-changer.

Barcelona FC recognized Messi's extraordinary contributions and held him in the highest regard. In March 2007, the club renewed his contract, ensuring his continued association with the team. His wages were increased to a level that could only be described as a king's ransom, highlighting the immense value he brought to the club.

Messi's journey from substitute to superstar was an extraordinary one, filled with remarkable performances and record-breaking achievements. His undeniable talent and unwavering dedication had earned him a place among the footballing elite, solidifying his status as one of the greatest players of his generation.
The revelation of Messi's new contract left most people utterly astounded, primarily due to the striking resemblance between his goal-scoring prowess and that of the legendary Diego Maradona. This led to the

emergence of the term "Messidona," as fans couldn't help but draw parallels between the two football icons. In a display of sheer brilliance, Messi further solidified his likeness to Maradona by nearly replicating two of his most iconic records in an astonishingly short span of just three weeks.

One such moment occurred during a Copa del Rey semi-final clash against Getafe on April 18th. In a jaw-dropping display of skill, Messi executed a goal reminiscent of Maradona's legendary strike in the 1986 FIFA World Cup quarter-final, famously known as the "goal of the century." Starting from the right side near the halfway line, Messi embarked on a mesmerizing 60-meter run, effortlessly evading the challenges of five defenders before delivering a perfectly angled finish, mirroring Maradona's feat in every aspect.

Not content with just one homage, Messi continued to showcase his uncanny resemblance to Maradona in a match against Espanyol on June 9th. In a moment that left spectators spellbound, Messi replicated Maradona's infamous "Hand of God" goal with remarkable precision.

This audacious act of using his hand to score left fans in awe, as they witnessed Messi channeling the very essence of Maradona's audacity and ingenuity.

These remarkable achievements served as a testament to Messi's extraordinary talent and his ability to emulate the greatness of Maradona. The world of football stood in awe as Messi left an indelible mark on the sport, solidifying his place among the all-time greats and etching his name alongside the illustrious Maradona.

Lionel Messi's remarkable performance on February 27th, 2007, during his 100th match for Barcelona against Valencia CF in the Champions League, solidified his place in football history. Displaying immense skill and determination, Messi not only scored an astonishing six goals but also provided an assist before being forced to leave the game prematurely due to yet another unfortunate muscle tear. This injury marked the fourth time within three seasons that Messi had encountered the same setback, highlighting the physical toll his relentless efforts had taken on his body.

Despite his recurring injuries, Messi's contributions to Barcelona remained exceptional throughout those three seasons. In a display of unrivaled talent, he managed to net an impressive 16 goals and provide 13 assists across all matches. However, during the 2008 to 2009 League matches, Messi faced a series of injuries that tested his resilience. Despite serious warnings from the medical staff, then-manager Rijkaard decided to field Messi, potentially due to perceived pressure from the club. This decision sparked concerns among some Barcelona players, who believed that the club was pushing Messi to play in every match, disregarding his well-being.

The consequences of this decision became evident as Barcelona concluded the 2008 season without any trophies and suffered an early exit in the Champions League, falling at the semi-finals against Manchester United. This disappointing outcome left Barcelona with a third-place finish in the league. The events of that season not only exposed the strain Messi endured but also raised questions about the club's prioritization of success over the welfare of their star player.

Nevertheless, Messi's outstanding performances and dedication to the game continued to captivate fans worldwide, cementing his status as one of the greatest footballers of all time.

The 2008-2009 season proved to be a pivotal moment in Messi's career, as Barcelona FC realized the need for a transformation in their style of play after two disappointing seasons. In order to initiate this change, the club made the bold decision to part ways with both Rijkaard and Ronaldinho. As a result, Messi was entrusted with the prestigious number 10 jersey, previously worn by Ronaldinho, symbolizing the immense faith the club had in his abilities. To further solidify their commitment to him, Barcelona FC offered Messi a lucrative contract in July 2008, making him the highest paid player in the club's history.

However, amidst this newfound success, Messi was faced with a daunting challenge - frequent injuries. Having endured a sidelining period of eight months from 2006 to 2008, it was imperative for the club to find a solution to this recurring issue. Barcelona FC took a proactive approach by implementing innovative training, nutrition, and lifestyle regimens for Messi. Additionally, they went the extra mile by assigning him a personal physiotherapist who would accompany him during his international duties with Argentina's national team.

This comprehensive approach yielded remarkable results, as Messi remained injury-free for the next four years, enabling him to fully unlock his potential on the field. The combination of Barcelona FC's unwavering support, strategic changes in his lifestyle, and the diligent care provided by his personal physiotherapist allowed Messi to flourish and showcase his exceptional talents to the world.

By the conclusion of the exhilarating 2012 campaign, Lionel Messi had etched his name in football history with an awe-inspiring tally of 38 goals and 18 assists in a staggering 51 matches. Alongside the remarkable performances of Samuel Eto'o and Thierry Henry, Barcelona FC soared to unprecedented heights, netting an astonishing total of 100 goals in all competitions, a monumental feat for the club. Messi's extraordinary talent was on full display as he repeatedly notched hat-tricks, leaving opponents in awe of his unrivaled skill. Moreover, his indomitable spirit propelled Barcelona to triumph in La Copa del Rey, La Liga, and the illustrious Champions League. Barcelona will forever cherish Messi's invaluable contributions, which played an instrumental role in the club's unprecedented success.

During the unforgettable 2008-2009 season, Barcelona etched their name in Spanish football folklore by becoming the first-ever Spanish club to achieve the coveted Treble. Despite encountering a few setbacks due to injuries, Messi's sheer brilliance on the field during the 2008 season was nothing short of extraordinary. His awe-inspiring performances earned him the prestigious title of runner-up for both the Ballon d'Or and the FIFA World Player of the Year awards, an accolade he narrowly missed out on, with Cristiano Ronaldo taking the crown on both occasions. Nonetheless, Messi's exceptional talent and unwavering determination left an indelible mark on the sport, solidifying his status as one of the greatest footballers of all time.

The year 2009 proved to be an extraordinary and triumphant one for Barcelona, as they added the prestigious 2009 Club World Cup against Estudiantes to their already impressive collection of trophies, bringing their total title victories for that year to an astounding six. Under the guidance of their newly appointed coach, Pep Guardiola, the team witnessed Lionel Messi's remarkable evolution on the field. Initially positioned on the right wing, a role he had played during Frank Rijkaard's tenure, Messi now transformed into a false winger, granted the freedom to venture into the center at his own discretion. As the season progressed, Messi returned to his wing position, showcasing his exceptional skills and leading Barcelona to their first final on May 13th. The match against Atlético Bilbao resulted in a resounding 4-1 victory, securing the Copa del Rey title for Barcelona. With an impressive tally of 23 league goals in 2009, Barcelona claimed the La Liga championship and achieved their fifth double. However, their journey did not end there. Barcelona continued their unstoppable march, overpowering Bayern Munich in the quarterfinals with a remarkable 4-0 triumph. The pinnacle of their success came in Rome, where they dramatically defeated Manchester United with a 2-0 victory, thus clinching the European championship, and etching their name in history as the first Spanish team to achieve a treble.

The achievements attained by Barcelona FC during this period can only be described as miraculous blessings, not only for the club itself but also for their star player, Messi.

The remarkable success of the season resulted in Messi being rewarded with a brand-new contract, signed on the 18th of September 2009. This contract not only solidified his commitment to the club until 2016 but also came with a substantial increase in his salary, now amounting to a staggering 12 million Euros. Additionally, the contract included a jaw-dropping $250 million buyout clause, emphasizing the club's determination to keep their prized asset.

Barcelona FC's winning streak continued well into the second half of 2009, surpassing all expectations. Their dominance was exemplified by their historic achievement of winning the sextuple, a feat never before accomplished by any other club. This extraordinary triumph saw Barcelona FC secure six top-tier trophies throughout the year, a truly remarkable accomplishment. However, the pinnacle of their success was undoubtedly their monumental victory in the FIFA Club World Cup against Estudiantes on December 19th. This momentous win further solidified Barcelona FC's status as an unstoppable force in the world of football.

Despite Lionel Messi's small stature, childhood physical ailment, and repeated injuries, he is widely regarded as one of the greatest football players of all time by professional football fans and expert commentators. His exceptional talent and relentless dedication have propelled him to the top of the sport.

At the young age of 22, Messi made history by winning both the Ballon d'Or and the FIFA World Player of the Year with the largest voting margins ever seen for these prestigious awards. This remarkable achievement solidified his status as a true footballing legend.

In 2010, Messi continued to amaze with his incredible performances, particularly in the form of hat tricks. He showcased his exceptional skills and determination by scoring three goals in a single match against CD Tenerife, Valencia CF, and Real Zaragoza. This extraordinary feat made him the first Barcelona player to achieve back-to-back hat-tricks in La Liga.

Messi's ability to consistently deliver outstanding performances despite his physical limitations and setbacks is a testament to his unrivaled talent and unwavering passion for the game. He has undoubtedly left an indelible mark on the world of football and will forever be remembered as one of the greatest players to have ever graced the sport.

In an awe-inspiring display of talent, Messi delivered a breathtaking finale to the 2010 matches by singlehandedly netting an astonishing four goals against Arsenal in the prestigious Champions League. Such an extraordinary feat left even the opposition's Manager, Arsene Wenger, in complete admiration as he showered Messi with an unequivocal commendation. Wenger, astounded by Messi's unparalleled abilities, unequivocally proclaimed him as the unrivaled best player in the world, surpassing his contemporaries by a significant margin. Comparing Messi to a PlayStation, Wenger marveled at his uncanny ability to exploit every single mistake made by his adversaries, leaving them utterly helpless and powerless against his mesmerizing skills.

As the curtains drew close on the year, Messi's remarkable goal-scoring prowess continued to astound the footballing world. His relentless drive and unrivaled finesse allowed him to amass a staggering tally of 47 goals, leaving defenders trembling in his wake. Not only a prolific scorer, but Messi also showcased his selflessness and vision by providing 11 assists, amplifying his impact on the game, and solidifying his status as a complete player. With each match, Messi's genius shone brighter, leaving an indelible mark on the annals of football history.

THE IMPRESSIVE SKILLS OF MESSI

Football requires a diverse range of abilities, encompassing dribbling, ball control, passing, scoring, defending, and tackling. Among the elite footballers, Lionel Messi stands out with his awe-inspiring skillset. His mastery over the game is unparalleled, evident in his effortless and stress-free dribbling, where he seamlessly manoeuvres the ball with precision. Messi's speed and agility while carrying the ball are remarkable, as if it is magnetically attached to his feet. Moreover, he possesses an exceptional instinct for scoring goals, effortlessly finding the back of the net. Not only does he possess incredible goal-scoring prowess, but he also possesses an astute vision, enabling him to spot and execute extraordinary passes, making him a remarkable playmaker on the field.

The comparison between Lionel Messi and Diego Maradona's skills is a topic frequently discussed by fans and commentators. While many argue that their skills are on par with each other, it can be contended that Messi has surpassed Maradona.

One notable aspect that supports this argument is the execution of the hand of God Goal. Although Maradona was the first to achieve this controversial feat, Messi also showcased his own version of it on October 4th, 2006 against Recreativo de Huerta. With incredible precision, Messi scored a goal obliquely with his hand, displaying his exceptional abilities on the field.

Furthermore, Messi's unstoppable nature is a recurring comment made by spectators and experts alike. His unparalleled dexterity in skillful dribbling, striking, and creating numerous scoring opportunities is a testament to his exceptional talent. Even in high stakes matches and against formidable opponents, Messi consistently displays his remarkable skills, further solidifying his superiority.

It is important to acknowledge that Messi's continuous display of dexterity and skill does not diminish the significance of his achievements. On the contrary, it highlights his genius and establishes him as a dominant force in the world of football. Messi's influence is at its peak, and he continues to amaze fans and experts with his extraordinary abilities.

The heart of the matter lies in the matter of the heart, and it is with utmost confidence, backed by extensive global research, that one can proclaim Messi as a true jinx-breaker, shattering countless records along his awe-inspiring journey. It is evident that this remarkable feat did not transpire overnight, but rather evolved progressively as Messi dedicated himself to mastering and showcasing the indispensable skills required for greatness.

Furthermore, it was in 2010 that Messi truly became the strategic centerpiece for Guardiola's team, a pivotal role that propelled his goal-scoring prowess to unprecedented heights. In that extraordinary season, Messi shattered an astonishing number of records, notching an impressive tally of 47 goals in regular competitions, matching Ronaldo's illustrious club record from the 1996-1997 season, before ascending to become Barcelona's all-time leading scorer in the prestigious Champions League.

Despite Barcelona's eventual elimination by Inter Milan, the crowned champions of 2010, Messi concluded the season as the top scorer for the second consecutive year, netting an astounding eight goals. His indomitable spirit and sheer determination were further exemplified by his status as the leading scorer in both the Spanish league and Europe, equaling Ronaldo's revered record with an astonishing 34 goals. This remarkable achievement played a pivotal role in Barcelona's triumphant conquest of La Liga, with the team suffering only a solitary defeat.

In essence, Messi's unwavering commitment to excellence, coupled with his relentless pursuit of greatness, has undeniably cemented his status as a jinx-breaker and record-breaker extraordinaire. His journey is a testament to the power of passion and dedication, proving that the heart truly is the driving force behind remarkable achievements.

Messi's impact on Barcelona FC's success story cannot be overstated. His numerous achievements have solidified his status as a game-changer and a key player in countless matches. One cannot discuss Barcelona FC's triumphs without acknowledging the pivotal role Messi has played.

One particular instance that showcases Messi's brilliance was during the 2010-2011 campaign. In the Super Copa de España, Messi's extraordinary performance led Barcelona to a resounding 4-0 victory over Sevilla, securing his first trophy of the season. Remarkably, this triumph came after a previous defeat, highlighting Messi's ability to bounce back and make a significant difference when it matters most.

Furthermore, Messi's exceptional playmaking skills were on full display during the El Clasico on November 29th, 2010, where Barcelona faced off against Jose Mourinho's Real Madrid. In a stunning 5-0 victory, Messi's contributions were instrumental in dismantling their fierce rivals. This match showcased Messi's ability to rise to the occasion and deliver exceptional performances against top-tier opponents.

Notably, Messi's impact extended beyond individual matches. He played a crucial role in Barcelona's record-breaking 16 consecutive league victories, a feat unparalleled in Spanish football. This remarkable achievement underlines Messi's ability to consistently perform at an exceptional level and propel his team to unparalleled success.

To cap off his exceptional season, Messi once again displayed his brilliance with a hat trick against Atlético Madrid on February 5th, 2011. This outstanding performance showcased his unmatched skill and determination, solidifying his worthiness of the accolades and trophies bestowed upon him.

In summary, Messi's contributions to Barcelona FC's success story are immeasurable. His unmatched talent, resilience, and ability to deliver exceptional performances in crucial moments have cemented his status as one of the greatest players in football history.

MESSI'S UNDERSTANDING OF THE GAME

The preceding discourse has provided evidence that Messi's journey as a professional football player has been characterized by an ongoing accumulation of invaluable experience. From the very inception of his career, he embarked on a path of continuous growth, gaining profound insights along the way. As time progressed, he gradually grasped the true essence of spending over an hour on the pitch, skilfully manoeuvring the ball amidst diverse circumstances, and expertly employing a multitude of strategies and tactics inherent to the game of football. Messi's profound understanding of the sport has evolved into a comprehensive mastery, allowing him to navigate the pitch with unparalleled finesse and expertise.

Without a shadow of a doubt, it is an undeniable truth that Messi's adoration for football knows no bounds, and in turn, the world of football showers him with an overwhelming affection. Any true enthusiast of the sport cannot help but be captivated by Messi, if not for his remarkable skills, then certainly for his unparalleled agility, lightning-quick reflexes, and an unstoppable drive that sets him apart from the rest.

Messi's exceptional talent and unparalleled achievements have solidified his position as the epitome of football greatness worldwide. With his iconic number 10 jersey always adorning his back, Messi's prowess as an attacking striker is simply unmatched. He possesses an uncanny ability to deliver awe-inspiring strikes that transcend the capabilities of any other player, while his masterful control of the ball allows him to execute precise passes with remarkable finesse.

Not only has Messi left an indelible mark on his club and country, but his contributions have also earned him the prestigious captain's armband for Argentina's national football team. Despite his countless accolades, including holding the Guinness World Record for the most goals scored in a single year, Messi's extraordinary skills suggest that he is destined to shatter numerous records in the years to come.

To truly grasp the sheer brilliance of Messi and the countless facets of his extraordinary talent, one must delve into his mesmerizing performances during the 2010 matches. This particular year stands as a testament to Messi's unparalleled efficiency and unrivalled prowess on the field. By closely examining a selection of his appearances in those matches, we gain profound insights into the enigmatic persona of this remarkable individual and the depths of his exceptional abilities. Undoubtedly, 2010 remains an indelible chapter in Messi's illustrious career, characterized by an astonishing level of productivity that has rarely been matched.

Messi's unrivaled talent on the football field has garnered unanimous acclaim from commentators, coaches, fans, sports analysts, and even his fellow colleagues, cementing his status as the premier footballer of our time. Many go as far as to hail him as not only one of the greatest players in history but potentially the greatest to have ever graced the sport.

In 2010, Messi's extraordinary performances for Barcelona FC propelled him to new heights, earning him the coveted inaugural FIFA Ballon d'Or. This prestigious accolade, a fusion of the esteemed Ballon d'Or and the FIFA World Player of the Year Award, recognized his exceptional skills, unmatched creativity, and sheer brilliance on the field.

However, even amidst this celebration of his individual brilliance, some critics voiced their discontent, pointing to Argentina's lack of success in the 2010 FIFA World Cup. Despite these dissenting opinions, Messi's undeniable impact and mesmerizing displays for Barcelona FC solidify his place among the footballing elite.

Despite Barcelona's loss in the Copa del Rey Final that year, Messi's performance in the Champions League was nothing short of remarkable. One particular moment stood out, as he executed an awe-inspiring dribble past three players, showcasing his incredible skills before attempting a shot on goal. Although he didn't manage to score on that mesmerizing play, Messi's impact on Barcelona would become even more evident later on when they faced Manchester United in the Champions League Final, securing their second consecutive appearance in the ultimate showdown. Once again, Messi emerged as the top scorer for the third year in a row, netting an impressive 12 goals. However, his true moment of glory came on May 28th, 2010, at Wembley, where he delivered a performance worthy of the man of the match title. It was during this game that he scored the match-winning goal, leading Barcelona to a resounding 3-1 victory. Messi's exceptional contributions throughout the season cannot be understated, as he concluded with an astonishing total of 53 goals and 24 assists in all competitions. This remarkable feat not only established him as Barcelona's all-time single-season top scorer but also made him the first player in Spanish football history to reach the prestigious 50-goal milestone.

In the year 2010, Lionel Messi truly astounded the world with his exceptional skills on the football field. He transformed himself into a remarkable combination of a playmaker, a prolific goal scorer, and a masterful goal creator. His versatility and proficiency in these roles were truly unmatched.

But it was during the 2011-2012 season that Messi reached new heights of greatness. He not only scored an astonishing 73 goals but also provided 29 assists, showcasing his ability to not only find the back of the net but also create scoring opportunities for his teammates. It seemed as if he had a supernatural ability to produce hat tricks, achieving this feat on more than ten occasions throughout the season.

Messi's impact extended beyond individual achievements. He played a pivotal role in helping Barcelona FC secure victories in both the Spanish and European super cups. In the Super Copa de España, he displayed his brilliance by scoring three goals, leading his team to a remarkable 5-4 triumph over their arch-rivals, Real Madrid. In doing so, he surpassed the legendary Raul as the competition's all-time top scorer, a testament to his unrivaled talent and relentless pursuit of excellence.

Lionel Messi's performances during this period were nothing short of extraordinary. His ability to seamlessly transition between different positions and fulfill the responsibilities of a number eight, a number nine, and a number ten was truly awe-inspiring. He not only dominated the game with his incredible goal-scoring prowess but also demonstrated his exceptional vision and ability to create opportunities for his teammates.

In summary, Lionel Messi's impact on the football world in 2010 and beyond cannot be overstated. His remarkable skills, record-breaking performances, and ability to lead his team to victory make him one of the greatest footballers of all time.

In the momentous year of 2010, specifically on the monumental day of December 18th, Lionel Messi showcased his unrivaled brilliance by scoring not once, but twice in the FIFA World Cup Finals. His extraordinary performance propelled Barcelona to a resounding 4-0 triumph over Santos, leaving no doubt about their superiority on the grandest stage of them all. As a testament to his exceptional abilities, Messi was bestowed with the prestigious Golden Ball, affirming his status as the most outstanding player in the tournament, a title he had already claimed two years prior.

The following year, 2011, proved to be yet another remarkable chapter in Messi's illustrious career. His relentless dedication and unparalleled skills were recognized once again when he was awarded the FIFA Ballon d'Or, an honor bestowed upon only the most exceptional footballers. By achieving this feat for the third time, Messi etched his name alongside the legendary Johan Cruyff, Michel Platini, and Marco van Basten, becoming only the fourth player in history to accomplish such a remarkable feat.

But Messi's achievements did not stop there. In that same year, he added another illustrious accolade to his ever-growing collection by clinching the UEFA Best Player in Europe Award. This remarkable triumph solidified his status as one of the greatest players to have ever graced the game, with football commentators, coaches, players, and fans alike placing him in the same revered category as the iconic Diego Maradona and Pelé, whose names are synonymous with football greatness.

With each passing year, Lionel Messi continues to redefine the boundaries of what is possible on the football pitch. His unrivaled talent, unwavering determination, and unparalleled success have firmly established him as a true legend of the sport, leaving an indelible mark on the annals of football history.

Given all these factors, it becomes abundantly clear that Messi is not just a skilled player, but also a master strategist who possesses an exceptional understanding of the intricacies and nuances of his sport. He comprehends the advantages and disadvantages within the game and skilfully utilizes them to his advantage. Moreover, Messi possesses the extraordinary ability to transform football into a captivating spectacle, ensuring that it is not merely a sport but an exhilarating form of entertainment. It is undeniable that football is meant to be savoured and relished, and in the presence of a player like Messi, one can only anticipate a plethora of mesmerizing and awe-inspiring moments on the field.

THE ASTONISHING ABILITIES OF MESSI

Lionel Messi's incredible talent surpasses the abilities of most professional footballers, earning him a place among the game's true legends. His skill set is so diverse and awe-inspiring that only a select few can even be mentioned here. When we talk about the "Greats" in football, we are referring to those players who have exhibited extraordinary and mind-boggling skills that are virtually impossible to replicate. Messi's prowess on the field is so unparalleled that even Coach Pep Guardiola himself declares that comparing him to other players is futile. In fact, Guardiola goes as far as expressing sympathy for those who aspire to challenge Messi's throne, as he believes it to be an unattainable feat. Messi is truly a one-of-a-kind talent, a unique force in the world of football.

Messi is not just an excellent player, but a sensational and truly one-of-a-kind talent. His extraordinary creativity and mind-blowing skills consistently unsettle his rivals, leaving them in awe. While he is a natural left-footer, his versatility is simply stunning, as he effortlessly excels in the middle or on either wing. However, Messi's ultimate comfort lies in positioning himself to unleash the power of his left leg, hence his preference for the right wing. Astonishingly, despite his shorter stature, his physique, combined with his innate speed and strength, allows him to outshine even the most formidable defenders. With unparalleled finesse, Messi elegantly manipulates the ball, making it seem as if it were magically attached to his feet.

Messi's extraordinary abilities never fail to astonish spectators as he effortlessly glides across the field, effortlessly manoeuvring the ball at an incredible speed. It's as if his boots possess an otherworldly magnetic attraction to the football. His addiction to scoring goals is undeniable, as he possesses an unparalleled instinct for finding the back of the net. Moreover, his exceptional vision enables him to effortlessly identify opportunities for both goal-scoring and creating plays, making him a true maestro on the field.

Messi's repertoire of skills extends far beyond his renowned dribbling prowess. With remarkable ease, he effortlessly manoeuvres the ball in any direction, even at lightning speed, as if it were bound to his feet by an invisible magnetic force. This mesmerizing display never fails to leave spectators in awe. Moreover, Messi's insatiable hunger for goals is undeniable. Possessing an uncanny ability to locate the goalpost with unwavering precision, he possesses a vision so astute that it borders on the supernatural. Whether it be scoring goals or orchestrating plays, Messi's exceptional peripheral vision enables him to effortlessly spot and execute the most intricate passes, leaving both teammates and opponents utterly astounded.

The discussion surrounding Messi's skills is endless, as the true extent of his capabilities remains unknown. Time and time again, Messi has proven to be a game changer when he enters the field as a substitute. He sees himself as a joker, much like the joker card in a deck, whose abilities have a profound impact on the flow of the game, leaving opposing players bewildered and unable to anticipate or comprehend his moves. Any player lacking tactical prowess in defending against Messi would undoubtedly be left astounded by his exceptional performance, characterized by his exceptional body control and an extensive repertoire of extraordinary skills.

Messi's reputation as a prolific goal scorer stem from a multitude of exceptional abilities that set him apart from his peers. His impeccable finishing, remarkable positioning, lightning-fast reactions, and astute ability to exploit defensive lines through well-timed attack runs are just a few reasons why he consistently finds the back of the net.

However, Messi's impact on the game extends far beyond his goal-scoring prowess. His playmaking skills are equally impressive, thanks to his exceptional vision and precise passing. He possesses a unique ability to orchestrate plays and create scoring opportunities for his teammates with unparalleled accuracy.

Furthermore, Messi's expertise in set pieces is truly awe-inspiring. Whether it's a free kick or a penalty kick, he displays unmatched proficiency in converting these opportunities into goals. His precision and finesse in these situations are nothing short of extraordinary.

While Messi's individual dribbling skills are widely acknowledged, it is during counterattacks that his true brilliance shines through. Employing tactical dribbling techniques, he effortlessly maneuvers the ball past opponents, leaving them helpless and mesmerized. Experts even go as far as to declare Messi the greatest dribbler of all time.

Diego Maradona, the legendary Argentine footballer, and former manager of Lionel Messi, eloquently proclaimed that Messi's ball control is beyond comparison, emphasizing that "the ball adheres to his foot as if it were glued." Having observed numerous exceptional players throughout his illustrious career, Maradona firmly asserts that Messi's mastery over the ball is unparalleled, placing him in a league of his own.

To put it simply, when we talk about Messi's goal-scoring abilities, we're only skimming the surface of his unparalleled skill set. His remarkable talent extends far beyond just finding the back of the net. His precision in finishing, his impeccable positioning on the field, his lightning-fast reactions, his strategic attack runs, his ability to create plays, his mastery of set pieces, and his unrivalled dribbling skills all combine to make him an extraordinary player. Many experts and fans alike hail him as the greatest of all time, a title that speaks volumes about his exceptional abilities on the pitch.

Messi's exceptional team playing skills are a perfect match for his extraordinary individual abilities. Renowned for his ability to create ingenious combinations, particularly with Barcelona's midfield maestros Xavi and Andrés Iniesta, Messi's versatility as a free attacking role player knows no bounds. Whether attacking from the wings or through the heart of the pitch, he effortlessly adapts to any position. From a tender age, his extraordinary gift blossomed as a prodigy, mesmerizing spectators with his innate ability to control the game as the enganche, a revered position in Argentine football. With his unrivalled playmaking skills, he effortlessly orchestrated the flow of the game, pulling the strings from the heart of the field, strategically positioning himself behind two formidable strikers. However, upon embarking on his career in Spain, he initially flourished as a left-winger or left side forward. It was under the guidance of manager Frank Rijkaard that Messi's position shifted to the right wing, a strategic move that allowed him to exploit the defense's vulnerabilities and infiltrate the central area of the field. This change provided him with ample opportunities to unleash his lethal left foot, either by taking audacious shots at goal or by delivering precise passes to his teammates.

During Pep Guardiola's tenure and subsequent managers, Messi's role on the field predominantly revolved around the false nine position, where he would often be deployed as a center forward or a lone striker. In this position, Messi showcased his versatility by constantly shifting towards the center, drifting into midfield, and luring defenders towards him. This strategic movement created ample space for passing, dribbling runs, and intricate combinations with his teammates, particularly Xavi and Iniesta.

However, under the guidance of Luis Enrique, Messi experienced a return to his earlier career days, resuming his position on the right wing. This shift allowed him to rediscover the dynamic and influential role he had previously excelled in. Simultaneously, when representing his national team, Argentina, Messi adapted to the tactics employed by various managers. Sometimes, he operated as a false nine, continuing to deceive opponents with his deceptive positioning. On other occasions, he donned the iconic number 10 jersey, assuming the role of an attacking midfielder, orchestrating the team's offensive maneuvers.

To delve deeper into the extraordinary abilities of Lionel Messi, it is highly recommended to analyse and appreciate his talents from various angles. By exploring Messi's capabilities through different perspectives, we can gain a comprehensive understanding of his brilliance and uncover the true extent of his skills.

EXPLORING MESSI'S ROLE AS A STRIKER

A striker in football is an integral member of a team, responsible for leading the attack and finding the back of the net. However, there exists a league of extraordinary players within this position, and Lionel Messi undoubtedly reigns supreme. His unparalleled ability to score goals surpasses that of ordinary strikers, making him a true force to be reckoned with on the field. Messi's exceptional talent and achievements make him a role model worth emulating, as he has not only revolutionized the game but has also opened boundless opportunities for aspiring players. By showcasing that the development of football skills is an ongoing journey, Messi has shattered the notion of limits and demonstrated that with dedication and perseverance, one can become a true master in any field they choose.

The 2011-2012 season marked an extraordinary milestone in Messi's illustrious career, surpassing all previous years in terms of sheer brilliance and captivating play. His performances on the field were nothing short of spectacular, leaving fans and pundits in awe. Not only did he exhibit unmatched skill and finesse, but he also achieved remarkable feats in terms of goals and assists.

Scoring a staggering 50 goals, Messi claimed the coveted title of La Liga's top goal scorer for the second time, solidifying his position as one of the greatest footballers of all time. Moreover, his ability to create opportunities for his teammates was equally impressive, as he registered an impressive tally of 16 assists, making him the league's second-best assist provider, falling just behind Mesut Ozil, who managed 17 assists.

Not content with dominating the domestic league, Messi's prowess extended to the grand stage of the UEFA Champions League. In a display of unrivaled consistency, he clinched the top scorer title for the fourth consecutive time, netting an astounding 14 goals. Additionally, he showcased his playmaking abilities by contributing 5 assists, establishing himself as one of the tournament's most influential players.

By the end of the season, Messi's remarkable tally stood at an astonishing 73 goals and 29 assists across all club competitions. This remarkable feat etched his name in the annals of football history, surpassing the records set by any other player in the professional football realm. Messi's unparalleled combination of goal-scoring prowess and creative playmaking made the 2011-2012 season an unparalleled pinnacle in his extraordinary career.

It is important to highlight the remarkable feat achieved by Lionel Messi in 2012, as he shattered all previous records by scoring an unprecedented 91 goals. This extraordinary accomplishment surpassed the legendary Gerd Muller's long-standing record of 85 goals set back in 1972. Messi's exceptional performance on the field not only made history but also solidified his position as one of the greatest footballers of all time.

Such an outstanding display of talent did not go unnoticed by Barcelona FC, who recognized Messi's invaluable contributions to their success. As a result, the club decided to extend their contract with this football prodigy until 2018, ensuring his continued presence and influence within the team. This decision reflects the immense trust and belief that Barcelona has in Messi's abilities, as they acknowledge his pivotal role in their ongoing pursuit of glory.

In a historic display of dominance, it was in the month of March in 2013 when Lionel Messi etched his name into the annals of football history. With unwavering determination and unparalleled skill, he accomplished a feat that had eluded every player before him. Messi's remarkable prowess allowed him to find the back of the net in an astounding 19 consecutive La Liga games, a record that seemed insurmountable. What set this achievement apart was not just the sheer number of goals, but the remarkable way he achieved them.

Throughout this extraordinary run, Messi showcased the very essence of his captivating game play, leaving spectators in awe and opponents in despair. With lightning speed that seemed to defy the laws of physics, he effortlessly glided past defenders, leaving them grasping at thin air. His agility and nimbleness on the field were matched only by his raw strength, making it an arduous task for any adversary to dispossess him of the ball. Messi's ability to shield the ball with an iron grip, even in the face of relentless pressure, was a testament to his unrivaled determination and unrivaled skill.

What made Messi's achievement truly remarkable was that he managed to score against every single team in the league during this mesmerizing run. No defense, no matter how formidable, could stifle his relentless pursuit of greatness. With each goal, he etched his name into the record books, forever etching his legacy as the first player to achieve such a remarkable feat.

In those unforgettable moments, Messi not only showcased his extraordinary speed and strength, but also his innate ability to bring joy and excitement to the beautiful game. His mesmerizing dribbles, lightning-quick bursts of acceleration, and unstoppable finishing ability captivated audiences worldwide. Messi's game play was a symphony of elegance and power, a testament to his unparalleled talent and dedication to his craft.

In March of 2013, Lionel Messi left an indelible mark on football history, cementing his status as one of the greatest players to ever grace the pitch. His record-breaking feat, scoring in 19 consecutive La Liga games against every team, was a testament to his exceptional speed, strength, and unrivaled skill. The world watched in awe as Messi defied the odds, captivating hearts and minds with his breathtaking displays. In those moments, he reminded us all of the sheer beauty and entertainment that his game play brings to the world of football.

There is simply no match for Messi when it comes to his unrivalled ability to create opportunities and deliver the perfect ball for that crucial final strike or game-changing assist. His extraordinary talent in dribbling is nothing short of awe-inspiring, leaving defenders in utter disbelief as he effortlessly weaves his way through them. Moreover, his cross-field passing is executed with such precision and accuracy that it becomes a formidable challenge for any opponent to thwart Messi's incredible exploits on the field.

MESSI'S ROLE AS A PLAYMAKER

There is no denying that Messi possesses an exceptional talent for creating opportunities on the field. However, it leaves everyone perplexed as to how he manages to maintain his status as the best player, even when he doesn't find the back of the net. One explanation that has already been touched upon is Messi's extraordinary ability to deliver pinpoint accurate passes, providing his teammates with golden opportunities to score. It is unfortunate that society tends to fixate solely on goals, as if they are the sole measure of a player's worth. In truth, assists should be esteemed even higher than goals. In terms of quality, Messi not only consistently provides assists but also finds the back of the net frequently. Furthermore, he orchestrates ball possession for his team, ensuring they maintain control of the game. What truly sets him apart is his unwavering composure and poise in any given situation. Messi remains unflustered, cool-headed, and in complete control, regardless of the circumstances.

The question that demands our attention is this: If a player has managed to achieve a remarkable feat of 40 league assists in a single season, does that not categorize them as the epitome of a true playmaker? Such an extraordinary accomplishment deserves nothing short of immense recognition, and it is only fitting to bestow upon this player a staggering 10 Ballons d'Or for their unrivalled performance. Similarly, if a player has the astonishing ability to score 40 league goals within a single season, it is an achievement that surpasses all expectations. To emphasize the sheer brilliance of this accomplishment, there is no denying that Lionel Messi should undoubtedly be hailed as the most exceptional player in the entire world.

Despite Messi's unparalleled skills as a playmaker-forward on the football field, truly comprehending his character as an individual necessitates delving into the multitude of aspects that shape his life away from the game. This sentiment was further reinforced by none other than the legendary Diego Maradona himself, who, following Messi's remarkable hat-trick in Barcelona's thrilling 3-3 draw against Real Madrid, emphatically proclaimed:

"I bear witness to the player who shall seamlessly succeed me in the realm of Argentinian football, and he is none other than the prodigious Messi. Messi, an extraordinary talent, possesses an inexhaustible potential that knows no bounds. With an impeccable skill set and an indomitable spirit, he embodies all the qualities required to ascend to the pinnacle of Argentina's footballing pantheon, ultimately surpassing all who came before him."

Not only did Maradona make a comment about Lionel Messi, but it is important to highlight that Messi has far exceeded Maradona's prediction. Just a little over a year later, Messi achieved one of the most unforgettable and historically significant goals of his entire career. While Maradona had famously scored his goal against England in the 1986 World Cup, Messi replicated that iconic moment by dribbling past five players and the goalkeeper from the halfway line to score a mind-blowing goal against Getafe in the 2006-2007 Copa del Rey. This extraordinary feat left even Anderson Luís de Souza, also known as Deco, with no other option but to acknowledge its greatness, admitting, "These are the goals that etch themselves into the annals of history. It is, without a doubt, the most breathtaking goal I have ever witnessed."

Arsene Wenger, the esteemed manager of Arsenal FC, boldly posed and promptly settled two profound questions: "Who reigns as the supreme player in the world? Lionel Messi. Who stands as the unrivalled player of all time? Lionel." The sheer brilliance and innate perfection of Lionel Messi may never be replicated, a sentiment shared by numerous football legends. Moreover, despite being a mere 28 years old, Messi's potential remains boundless, as legendary players continue to astound and inspire even at this age. Undeniably, Messi's greatness transcends the confines of time and eras, leaving an indelible mark on the sport of football.

MESSI'S SCORING PROWESS

Goals and assists hold an indomitable significance in any discourse surrounding present-day football matches or the illustrious chronicles of this sport. Specifically, in relation to Lionel Messi's unyielding magnificence, it becomes abundantly clear that goals and assists are fundamental components that define his exceptional prowess.

At the tender age of 21, Lionel Messi made a significant change by exchanging his cherished number 19 jersey for the iconic number 10 at Barcelona FC. This coveted number became available due to the departure of the legendary Ronaldinho. In the following years, Messi's incredible talent and dedication propelled him to achieve extraordinary milestones.

In a span of 110 matches, Messi's awe-inspiring performance led to an astonishing 42 goals, making him an integral part of Barcelona's success. During this period, he clinched two La Liga titles, two Super Copa titles, and even triumphed in the prestigious Champion's League. His impact on the field was undeniable, leaving fans and critics in awe of his exceptional abilities.

Since the 2008-2009 season, Messi has continued to mesmerize the football world with his extraordinary skills. Having played in an impressive 372 matches for Barcelona, he has showcased his remarkable goal-scoring prowess, netting an astounding 370 goals. Not only has he been a prolific scorer, but he has also displayed his selflessness by providing no less than 100 assists for his teammates.

Messi's remarkable goals have played a pivotal role in Barcelona's dominance, contributing to an impressive five La Liga titles. His extraordinary performances on the pitch have not gone unnoticed, as he has been honored with a record-breaking four consecutive Ballons d'Or awards. This unprecedented achievement solidifies his status as one of the greatest footballers of all time.

In summary, Lionel Messi's decision to switch to the number 10 jersey marked the beginning of an illustrious career filled with countless accolades and achievements. His goal-scoring prowess, selflessness, and unwavering dedication have not only led to personal success but have also propelled Barcelona to numerous triumphs on both domestic and international stages.

It is imperative that we do not underestimate the remarkable achievements of Lionel Messi, as he has etched his name in the prestigious Guinness World Records. One such awe-inspiring feat is his record-breaking tally of 91 goals in a single year, encompassing both his club and national team performances. This extraordinary milestone not only solidifies Messi's position as a footballing legend but also sets him apart from his peers.

Furthermore, Messi shares a joint record of 25 goals with the renowned Vivian Woodward, further exemplifying his incredible scoring prowess. Additionally, he shares the record for the most goals in FIFA Club World Cup history, a commendable achievement achieved alongside the esteemed Danilson and Mohammed Aboutrika, with each player netting a total of four goals.

Moreover, Messi's consistency and ability to find the back of the net are unparalleled, as evidenced by his record of scoring in the most consecutive league matches. In a staggering display of skill and determination, he managed to score an astonishing 30 goals in just 19 matches, leaving spectators in awe of his unrivaled talent.

It is also worth highlighting Messi's exceptional performance during the 2006-2007 season, where he left an indelible mark by scoring 14 goals in 26 appearances.

This remarkable display of goal-scoring prowess further solidifies his status as one of the greatest footballers of all time.

In conclusion, Lionel Messi's Guinness World Records serve as a testament to his extraordinary abilities and unrivaled impact on the world of football. His incredible goal-scoring records, both individually and collectively, showcase his unparalleled talent and firmly establish him as a true maestro of the beautiful game.

In 2007, Lionel Messi reached a significant milestone in his career as he played his 100th match for Barcelona. However, this season was plagued by a muscle tear, which greatly affected his performance. Despite this setback, Messi managed to scrape by with a commendable tally of 16 goals and 13 assists.

Fast forward to 2009, and we witnessed a complete transformation in Messi's game. This season proved to be a turning point for him, as he showcased his extraordinary skills by notching an impressive total of 38 goals and 18 assists. It was a remarkable display of his talent and marked a new era for the young football prodigy.

But it was the year 2010 that Messi will forever cherish as his most fruitful period. This was the year of the hat-trick for him, where he accomplished an astonishing feat of scoring 47 goals and providing 11 assists. It was a truly exceptional performance that solidified his status as one of the greatest footballers of all time.

The following season, 2010-2011, brought even greater glory for Messi. His remarkable abilities continued to shine as he amassed a staggering count of 53 goals and 24 assists across all competitions. Once again, Messi's incredible output surpassed all expectations and set new records that seemed almost impossible to achieve.

Throughout these remarkable seasons, Lionel Messi consistently raised the bar and established himself as a record-breaking force in the world of football. His unwavering determination, coupled with his unparalleled skills, propelled him to new heights and solidified his place among the legends of the sport.

In the year 2012, Lionel Messi's remarkable goal-scoring prowess reached unprecedented heights, as he shattered

Gerd Muller's long-standing record of 85 goals by achieving an astonishing tally of 91 goals. This extraordinary feat not only solidified Messi's status as an exceptional player but also highlighted his unrivaled ability to find the back of the net consistently. Additionally, this remarkable achievement marked his 19th consecutive game in La Liga with a goal, further cementing his reputation as the epitome of excellence in the world of football. It is without a doubt that Messi's unparalleled skill as both a player and a goal scorer set him apart from his peers, making him undeniably the best among the rest.

MESSI'S DRIBBLING PROWESS

Messi's mastery of dribbling is without a doubt his greatest asset on the field. With remarkable ease and finesse, he effortlessly manoeuvres past defenders, showcasing a level of versatility that seems boundless. Despite the misconception among fans and commentators that his dribbling prowess is innate, it is important to recognize the countless hours of rigorous training that Messi dedicated to honing this skill from the start of his professional career. Nonetheless, Messi's mesmerizing displays on the field often give the impression that his extraordinary dribbling abilities come naturally to him.

According to Pranav Neuer, defending against Messi's dribbling skills is akin to witnessing a mesmerizing three-act magic trick. Neuer compares this spectacle to the structure of a magic trick, which comprises three distinct parts or acts. The first act, known as "the pledge," involves the magician presenting something ordinary. Similarly, when Messi initiates his run towards the defender, he does so at a seemingly minimal pace, luring them into a false sense of security. The defender, unaware of the impending danger, may initially back off gently or simply hold their ground, as there appears to be no immediate cause for concern. This familiar scenario resembles countless previous encounters with other attackers. As Messi gradually closes in on the defender's territory, he entices them to engage with the ball, almost as if he's inviting them to challenge him and attempt to win it. However, it becomes evident that Messi's true intention is far from relinquishing possession easily.

In the mesmerizing second act known as "The Turn," the magician effortlessly transcends the realm of the ordinary and delves into the extraordinary. With a graceful shift of his body weight onto his left side, he glides away from you, leaving you captivated and searching for an explanation. Your mind is devoid of rational thought, for you are filled with unwavering confidence that you possess the skills to track his every move and seize the ball with the might of your dominant right foot. You understand he intends to bewilder you, yet you resist the urge to applaud prematurely, patiently awaiting the moment when he stumbles, when his touch becomes too heavy. And then, with a surge of determination, you decide that the time has come to intercept his path, extending your right leg forward like a majestic eagle soaring in pursuit of its prey.

That is the moment when he executes the third act, the most challenging and awe-inspiring part of the game, known as "The Prestige." As you position your right foot in anticipation, little do you know that his brilliance surpasses your expectations. In a split second, with a flick of his foot, he effortlessly places the ball in the tiniest pocket of space between your grounded right foot and the approaching defender, whom he has already targeted. With astonishing speed and agility, he gracefully leaps and glides over your attempted challenge, aided by his remarkably low center of gravity, allowing him to regain control of both his composure and the ball. Once he has fully mastered the situation, he proceeds to outmanoeuvre the next opponent, and then the next, continuing this mesmerizing display. All you can do is witness the sight of his number 10 jersey, emblazoned with the name "MESSI," as he leaves you in his wake."

Pranav Neuer, an astute observer of the game, meticulously delves into the intricate artistry behind Messi's dribbling prowess, providing a comprehensive account from the perspective of a defender. Neuer's vivid depiction not only unveils the remarkable array of skills that Messi possesses, but also offers a profound understanding of the sheer brilliance he brings to the realm of football gameplay.

MAGNIFICENT MESSI'S FREE KICK

Lionel Messi, the extraordinary soccer prodigy hailing from South America, has earned global acclaim for his unparalleled mastery of the game, astonishing speed that defies belief, and mesmerizing dribbling techniques that leave even the most seasoned defenders spellbound. Yet, amidst this tapestry of remarkable talent, there exists a facet of his prowess that demands utmost admiration: his remarkable ability to score free-kick goals, an artistry that firmly establishes him among the pantheon of soccer's all-time greats.

The recent news of Messi surpassing the legendary Brazilian goalkeeper Rogério Ceni in free-kick goals serves as an awe-inspiring testament to his unrivalled prowess on the field. Having scored an astonishing 65 free-kick goals throughout his illustrious career, Messi showcases an extraordinary level of precision, consistently finding the perfect angle to outsmart and outmanoeuvre the world's most formidable goalkeepers. This remarkable feat solidifies Messi's status as a true maestro, capable of bending the laws of physics to his will and leaving spectators in awe of his unparalleled skill and accuracy.

Messi's numerous accomplishments are undeniably remarkable, but one that stands out above all others is his unparalleled supremacy at Barcelona, where he astoundingly netted a staggering total of 672 official goals. This extraordinary feat solidifies his status as the greatest goal-scorer for a single club in the entire history of soccer, when considering official matches. Throughout his extensive and fruitful tenure with the Catalan club, Messi not only amassed an impressive collection of titles but also created an abundance of enchanting moments, with a significant number originating from his flawlessly executed free-kick strikes. These magical instances served as a testament to his exceptional skill and precision, leaving spectators in awe of his unrivalled talent.

Lionel Messi, undeniably one of the most extraordinary footballers to grace the field, transcends the realm of greatness by showcasing an unparalleled mastery in the delicate art of scoring free-kick goals. His sheer brilliance and unwavering adaptability in the face of diverse challenges elevate him to the status of a living legend within the realm of this beloved sport. As the chapters of his illustrious career unfold, the mere contemplation of what further heights he may scale and the enchanting moments he will gift us with fills our hearts with anticipation. Messi, an unequivocal gem in the vast tapestry of soccer, is destined to radiate his mesmerizing brilliance for countless years to come, leaving an indelible mark on the annals of the beautiful game.

MESSI No. 10

Argentina has recently unveiled an incredibly unique and unconventional strategy to pay homage to the legendary football icon Lionel Messi upon his retirement. The nation's plan, which has left the world astonished, aims to celebrate the incomparable achievements of Messi in an unprecedented manner.

Argentine Football Association president Claudio Tapia has made a resolute declaration that, once Lionel Messi decides to hang up his boots in the Argentina national team, he will ensure that no other player will have the honour of donning the iconic No. 10 jersey for the Albiceleste ever again. Tapia's unwavering commitment to preserving Messi's legacy in the national team is a testament to the indelible mark the legendary player has left on Argentine football. By retiring the No. 10 shirt, Tapia aims to immortalize Messi's unparalleled contributions and ensure that his extraordinary talent remains etched in the hearts of football fans for generations to come.

Tapia made a resolute declaration during a highly anticipated press conference, vowing to honour the legendary Lionel Messi in an unprecedented manner. As the Argentine football icon contemplates retirement from the national team, Tapia asserted that no other player shall ever don the sacred number 10 jersey once Messi hangs it up. In an awe-inspiring tribute to Messi's unparalleled contributions to the sport, Tapia proclaimed that this iconic number shall be forever retired, serving as an everlasting symbol of reverence and gratitude towards the maestro. Tapia emphasized that this gesture is merely the minimum gesture of appreciation that they can extend to the footballing virtuoso, who has left an indelible mark on the nation's footballing legacy.

In a conversation with Zidane for Adidas, Messi expressed his thoughts on the significance of the number 10 shirt. While acknowledging that its importance may have diminished over time, Messi still recognizes its special status. Reflecting on his time in Paris, where he didn't wear the number 10 shirt, Messi admitted that he missed having his iconic number. Wearing the number 10 had become a part of his identity, both with Barcelona and the national team. However, he quickly adapted to wearing the number 30, which also held sentimental value for him as it was the number he started playing with. Zidane, on the other hand, emphasized that for fans, seeing Messi in the number 10 shirt is what truly matters. He believes that the number 10 has become synonymous with Messi and that seeing him on the field wearing that number brings immense joy to spectators.

MESSI AND FC BARCELONA

The 6th of November 2003 will forever be etched in the annals of FC Barcelona as a momentous day. It marked the debut of a football prodigy who would go on to become the greatest player to ever don the iconic Barcelona jersey, and quite possibly, any football jersey in existence. At the tender age of 16, a young and awe-inspiring Leo Messi graced the pitch as a substitute in a friendly match against Porto, where he had the honour of inaugurating the Portuguese club's state-of-the-art stadium, Do Dragão. This extraordinary event not only solidified Messi's place in history but also foreshadowed the incredible legacy he would build in the years to come.

The Sporting Director of FC Barcelona stepped in to address Messi's challenging situation when he was diagnosed with a growth hormone deficiency at the tender age of eleven.

Displaying immense compassion and foresight, Carles Rexach not only offered to cover Messi's medical expenses but also presented a remarkable proposition. He pledged to take care of the medical bills on the condition that Messi would relocate to Spain in the future to enhance his football career. This pivotal moment marked the beginning of Messi's extraordinary journey as he was warmly embraced into the prestigious Barcelona Youth Academy.

Messi's journey to greatness was nothing short of remarkable as he consistently showcased his exceptional skills and talent at every stage of his development. From a young age, he displayed immense potential, rapidly ascending the ranks from Barca C to Barca B, and ultimately securing a spot in the prestigious first team at an unprecedented pace.

During his meteoric rise, Messi reached a significant milestone during the 2003/2004 season when he celebrated his 16th birthday. This special occasion coincided with his team's participation in a friendly match against Porto, which happened to be the inaugural game held at the newly constructed Dragao Stadium. It was a momentous event that marked Messi's official debut with the team, where he left a lasting impression with his breathtaking performance.

Not content with just friendly matches, Messi's hunger for success led him to make his first appearance in an official match on October 16, 2004. This significant moment occurred during Barcelona's highly anticipated derby clash against Espanyol at the iconic Olympic Stadium. In a thrilling encounter, Messi's impact was undeniable as he played a crucial role in securing a triumphant victory for his team, with a final score of 0-1.

These early milestones in Messi's career not only demonstrated his exceptional abilities but also foreshadowed the incredible achievements he would go on to accomplish. It was clear that Messi was destined for greatness, and these breakthrough moments served as a mere glimpse into the extraordinary journey that lay ahead for the young prodigy.

Due to a significant number of key players sustaining serious injuries, the reserve team players were called upon to step up and fill the void in the first team. Seizing this golden opportunity, Messi made the most of his regular inclusion in the Barcelona squads.

On the momentous day of May 1, 2005, a mere 17 years, 10 months, and 7 days into his young life, Lionel Messi etched his name in football history as the youngest player ever to score a league goal for FC Barcelona, defying all expectations. This remarkable feat occurred during a thrilling encounter against Albacete, showcasing Messi's extraordinary talent and precocious abilities at such a tender age.

However, it was Messi's awe-inspiring performance in the Joan Gamper Trophy match against Juventus that truly catapulted him into the global spotlight. In a resounding 3-0 victory over the formidable Chelsea at the renowned Stamford Bridge, Messi's breakthrough moment left spectators and pundits alike stunned. Despite facing numerous setbacks due to injuries, Messi's indomitable spirit propelled him to play a remarkable 17 games, including six in the prestigious Champions League and two in the fiercely contested Copa del Rey.

Unleashing his true potential in the following season, Messi elevated his game to unprecedented heights, leaving the world in awe of his unparalleled skill and artistry. One goal stood out as a testament to his genius – a mesmerizing strike against Getafe in the Copa del Rey. This extraordinary display of talent solidified Messi's status as a force to be reckoned with and served as a harbinger of the greatness that was yet to come from this prodigious football prodigy.

Despite failing to win any titles in the 2006/2007 season, Messi's exceptional performance did not go unnoticed. He secured second place in the FIFA World Player awards and an impressive third place in the Ballon d'Or rankings. The following season, 2007/08, Messi continued to dazzle on the field, scoring an impressive 16 goals and providing ten assists in 40 games. His outstanding performance earned him the runner-up position for the FIFA World Player Award for the second consecutive year in 2008. However, it was in the 2008/2009 season that Messi truly emerged as the shining star of Barcelona. Remarkably injury-free throughout the entire season, he showcased his unparalleled skills in 51 games, netting an astonishing 38 goals. Messi's remarkable rise to prominence was undeniable, solidifying his position as one of the greatest players in the world.

The Argentinian superstar not only played a crucial role in the Copa del Rey and Champions League finals, but also emerged as the hero by scoring Barcelona's second goals in both matches. His exceptional performance in 2009 earned him the prestigious FIFA World Player and Ballon d'Or awards. Furthermore, he showcased his remarkable goal-scoring abilities by becoming the top scorer of the league in the 2009-2010 season, matching the historic record set by Ronaldo in 1996-1997 with an impressive tally of 34 goals.

Messi's influence continued to grow as he delivered the winning goal against Estudiantes, securing Barcelona's first-ever World Cup victory. The following season, he took his game to another level, astonishingly netting a staggering 53 official goals, a Spanish record that was only matched by the equally talented Cristiano Ronaldo. Messi's unrivaled talent and consistent brilliance truly set him apart as one of the greatest footballers of all time.

In an incredible display of talent and skill, he etched his name in football history by winning the prestigious Ballon d'Or for the third time in 2011. This remarkable achievement had only been accomplished by a select few legends of the game, including Cruyft, Platini, and Van Basten. However, he didn't stop there. In a stunning display of dominance, he went on to become the first player ever to claim the coveted award four times.

His exceptional performances continued to captivate the world in the years to come. In both 2013 and 2014, he narrowly missed out on the top spot, finishing second among the world's finest footballers. Nevertheless, his impact on the game remained unrivaled.

During the 2011/2012 season, Messi's brilliance reached new heights as he surpassed Cesar Rodriguez's long-standing record of 232 goals. These astonishing numbers solidified his place as a true legend of the sport, and his records in Barcelona still stand unbroken, a testament to his unparalleled skill and dedication.

Beyond individual accolades, his contributions to his club, Barcelona, have been nothing short of extraordinary. With an impressive tally of six League titles, three Champions League titles, and two Spanish Cup titles, he has played an instrumental role in the team's success. Additionally, he has lifted the UEFA Super Cup title twice, clinched six Spanish Super cup titles, and triumphed in the FIFA Club World Cup on two occasions.

As we look back on his illustrious career, his impact on the world of football is immeasurable. With a record-breaking number of Ballon d'Or wins, unmatched goal-scoring prowess, and an extensive list of titles, he has solidified his status as one of the greatest players to ever grace the pitch.

2013/2014, 2012/2013, 2011/2012 ,2011/2012, 2011/2012, 2011-12 2011/2012, 2010/2011, 2010/2011, 2010/2011, 2009/2010, 2009/2010, 2009/2010, 2009/2010, 2008/2009, 2008/2009, 2008/2009, 2006/2007, 2005/2006, 2005/2006, 2005/2006, and 2004/2005.

The 2013/2014 season was a tumultuous one for Barcelona, as they encountered numerous setbacks that left their fans disheartened. Notably, they experienced bitter defeats in crucial matches, including the Copa del Rey semi-finals. Their journey in the Champions League was no less nerve-wracking, as AC Milan came dangerously close to eliminating them in the first knock-out round. However, Barcelona managed to turn the tide in the second leg, staging a remarkable 4-0 comeback, thanks to the incredible performance of their star player, Lionel Messi. With two goals and an assist from Messi, Barcelona not only snatched victory from the jaws of defeat but also reignited the hopes and dreams of their devoted supporters.

In his remarkable ninth season with Barcelona, Lionel Messi solidified his commitment to the club by signing a new contract on February 7th, 2016. This agreement not only extended his stay until 2018 but also saw his fixed wage skyrocket to an impressive 13 million Euros. Just a month later, on March 17th, Messi proudly donned the captain's armband in a league match against Rayo Vallecano, solidifying his status as the team's undisputed focal point. This level of influence was only rivalled by the great Barcelona legends of the past, such as Josep Samitier, Laszlo Kubala, and Johan Cruyff.

Since his transformation into a false nine three years prior, Messi's impact on the team's attacking prowess had grown exponentially. His contribution to goals soared from a respectable 24 percent during Barcelona's treble-winning campaign to an astonishing 40 percent in 2016. This statistical leap not only showcased Messi's exceptional skill and talent but also highlighted his crucial role in the team's success.

In awe of Messi's extraordinary abilities, Gerard Pique passionately declared that there is simply no match for him in the entire world of football. Pique emphasized that even during challenging times, when our team is struggling, it is imperative to rely on Messi's unparalleled talent. Astonishingly, even if he were to be hindered by an injury, his mere presence on the field has the power to elevate not only our spirits but also our overall performance as a team.

Over the course of an astounding 17 seasons, Lionel Messi adorned the iconic blaugrana jersey, etching his name in the annals of football history. With an unwavering commitment to FC Barcelona, he graced the pitch an astonishing 778 times, an unparalleled feat that stands as a testament to his unwavering dedication and enduring brilliance.

But it was not just his presence on the field that mesmerized fans worldwide; it was his ability to consistently find the back of the net with an awe-inspiring frequency. With an extraordinary tally of 672 goals, Messi propelled himself to the summit of the club's all-time scoring chart, leaving an indelible mark that may never be surpassed. Each goal, a masterpiece, showcased his mesmerizing skill, unfathomable precision, and an innate understanding of the beautiful game.

To comprehend the magnitude of his achievements, one must delve into the numbers. Averaging an astonishing 0.86 goals per match, Messi's scoring prowess was nothing short of breathtaking. Match after match, he defied the boundaries of what was deemed possible, leaving defenders helpless and goalkeepers in despair. His relentless pursuit of excellence transformed every game into a spectacle, each touch of the ball a potential moment of magic, and every goal a work of art.

Messi's tenure at FC Barcelona was not merely a period of dominance, but a golden era that will forever be etched in the memories of football enthusiasts. His unrivaled longevity, record-breaking appearances, and extraordinary goal-scoring ability have solidified his status as one of the greatest players to have ever graced the sport. The blaugrana jersey became a symbol of his unwavering loyalty, unmatched talent, and an unbreakable bond with the club and its adoring fans.

Competition	Titles	Seasons
La Liga (Spanish league)	10	2004/05, 2005/06, 2008/09, 2009/10, 2010/11, 2012/13, 2014/15, 2015/16, 2017/18, 2018/19
Copa del Rey (Spanish Cup)	7	2008/09, 2011/12, 2014/15, 2015/16, 2016/17, 2017/18, 2020/21
Supercopa de Espana (Spanish Super Cup)	7	2006, 2009, 2010, 2011, 2013, 2016, 2018
UEFA Champions League	4	2005/06, 2008/09, 2010/11, 2014/15
UEFA Super Cup	3	2009, 2011, 2015
FIFA Club World Cup	3	2009, 2011, 2015

In addition to his remarkable achievements at Barcelona, Lionel Messi has left an indelible mark on other prestigious clubs as well. His impact at Paris Saint-Germain cannot be understated, as he has already magnificently netted an astonishing 32 goals in just 75 appearances. Moreover, his recent stint at Inter Miami CF has been nothing short of sensational, with Messi already delivering eleven crucial goals. These exceptional numbers not only highlight his unwavering consistency but also epitomize his unparalleled adaptability to thrive in diverse teams and leagues.

MESSI AND ARGENTINA

Messi, the football prodigy, hailing from the vibrant nation of Argentina, has left an indelible mark on both the domestic and international stages. Born in the enchanting city of Rosario, Messi's contributions to his homeland's national game and international play have been nothing short of monumental. In every match he graces, Messi's presence is undeniable, captivating the attention of fans and opponents alike. With a mesmerizing display of unparalleled skills and talent, he effortlessly commands the pitch, leaving spectators in awe.

Yet, despite his numerous achievements, there is one elusive triumph that has eluded Messi throughout his illustrious career: lifting the prestigious World Cup trophy. This unfulfilled dream weighs heavily on Messi's heart, as he has experienced a tumultuous journey filled with both triumphs and setbacks. Initially, the Argentine nation was slow to embrace this young prodigy from Barcelona, but Messi's relentless pursuit of excellence gradually won over the hearts of his compatriots.

It is a bittersweet reality for Messi, knowing that he has not been granted the golden opportunity to hoist the coveted World Cup trophy. However, his unwavering determination and unwavering commitment to his craft continue to inspire and motivate him. Despite the challenges he has faced, Messi remains resolute, tirelessly striving to achieve the ultimate glory for his beloved Argentina.

In the grand tapestry of football history, Lionel Messi's name will forever be etched as one of the greatest players to have graced the sport. His legacy transcends borders, captivating the world with his extraordinary talent and unwavering dedication. As Messi continues to chase his World Cup dreams, the entire footballing community eagerly awaits the day when this extraordinary maestro finally claims his rightful place among the pantheon of World Cup champions.

Although Messi does not carry the entire burden of performance for Argentina, it is undeniable that his contributions have been significant even before his remarkable achievements in 2012. Despite not scoring as many goals as he desired, Messi has consistently displayed his prowess and played a crucial role for La Albiceleste. His inspiration from the legendary Maradona has been a driving force behind his dedication and determination. As Messi himself once revealed, Maradona's influence has been instrumental in shaping his football journey.

"During the pivotal year of 1993, as I began to forge my own path and develop my own thoughts, a remarkable figure had just made his triumphant return to his homeland - none other than the legendary Diego Maradona. Immersed in his awe-inspiring journey, my admiration for him grew exponentially. Joining the prestigious Newell's Old Boys after his stint in Spain, Maradona's presence was not only felt within the realm of club football but also as an integral member of the national team that secured qualification for the prestigious

USA '94 tournament. Undeniably, it was Maradona's indomitable spirit and unmatched talent that ignited a flame within me, serving as an unwavering source of inspiration as I embarked on my own journey in the world of football."

It comes as no surprise that Messi has consistently displayed exceptional performance, not only on the field but also in various aspects of his life. Drawing inspiration from an extraordinary mentor like Maradona, Messi's achievements speak volumes. His influence was instrumental in propelling his team to the finals and securing victory in the 2004/2005 FIFA World Youth Championship, as well as claiming the prestigious 2008 Summer Olympics Gold Medal. As we delve deeper into this essay, we will uncover the multitude of individual accolades that Messi would go on to receive throughout the following decade.

Messi, the esteemed captain of the Argentina National Team, has proven to be a true leader through his remarkable display of leading by example. His exceptional talent and precision have resulted in an astonishing ten free-kick goals for his beloved national squad. This extraordinary feat not only adds to his own illustrious legacy but also propels Argentine soccer to unprecedented heights, inspiring a new era of excellence.

Furthermore, he has garnered numerous prestigious accolades that serve as a testament to his exceptional talents and accomplishments. These commendations, bestowed upon him personally, further highlight his remarkable achievements and reinforce his standing as a highly esteemed individual:

Competition	Titles	Year
FIFA World Cup	1	2022
Finalissima (UEFA-CONMEBOL trophy)	1	2022
Copa America (South American title)	1	2021
Olympic gold medal	1	2008
FIFA Under-20 World Cup	1	2005

Maradona played a pivotal role in revolutionizing the world of football between 1976 and 1997, particularly during the latter stages of his illustrious career when he exhibited remarkable maturity on the field. However, it is Lionel Messi who has seamlessly taken up the baton and propelled the game into a new era over the past 20 years, displaying an unparalleled level of skill and consistency that shows no signs of waning. The abundance of statistical evidence overwhelmingly supports this resounding conclusion.

LET THE STATS SPEAK

ARGENTINA 2005-22

INTERNATIONAL GAMES	164
INTERNATIONAL GOALS	90
CLUB GAMES	862
CLUB GOALS	706
TROPHIES	37
WORLD CUP GAMES	19
WORLD CUP GOALS	6

LIONEL MESSI — FORWARD

MESSI: PERSONAL PROFILE	
Full name	Lionel Andrés Messi
Date of birth	24 June 1987 (1987-06-24)
Place of birth	Rosario, Argentina
Height	1.69 meters (5 feet, 7 inches)
Playing position	Forward

Countless "Best of Lionel Messi" videos serve as a testament to his consistent brilliance throughout his illustrious career. However, it is time to silence the debates and allow the undeniable power of statistics to paint the true picture.

Messi's prowess on the field cannot be overstated. Not only is he an exceptional goal scorer, but he also possesses an uncanny ability to create opportunities for his teammates. Since August 2009, Messi has netted an astonishing 375 goals for both his club and country, surpassing every goal record ever set within the same time frame in the history of the sport. His goal-scoring prowess alone sets him apart from his peers.

However, Messi's brilliance extends beyond scoring goals. His playmaking abilities are unparalleled, with an impressive tally of 142 assists and 815 key passes since August 2009. These numbers highlight his exceptional vision, precision, and ability to set up his teammates for success. No other forward even comes close to matching Messi's playmaking skills.

So, while it's true that Messi stands as the ultimate goal-scoring and playmaking force, it's worth delving into the statistics to truly comprehend the magnitude of his impact on the game.

Competition	Titles	Seasons
La Liga (Spanish league)	10	2004/05, 2005/06, 2008/09, 2009/10, 2010/11, 2012/13, 2014/15, 2015/16, 2017/18, 2018/19
Copa del Rey (Spanish Cup)	7	2008/09, 2011/12, 2014/15, 2015/16, 2016/17, 2017/18, 2020/21
Supercopa de Espana (Spanish Super Cup)	7	2006, 2009, 2010, 2011, 2013, 2016, 2018
UEFA Champions League	4	2005/06, 2008/09, 2010/11, 2014/15
UEFA Super Cup	3	2009, 2011, 2015
FIFA Club World Cup	3	2009, 2011, 2015

Honor	Titles	Seasons
Ligue 1 (French league)	2	2021/22, 2022/23
Trophee des Champions (French Super Cup)	1	2022

Competition	Titles	Year
FIFA World Cup	1	2022
Finalissima (UEFA-CONMEBOL trophy)	1	2022
Copa America (South American title)	1	2021
Olympic gold medal	1	2008
FIFA Under-20 World Cup	1	2005

Award	Titles	Year/Season
Ballon d'Or (World Player of the Year)	8	2009, 2010, 2011, 2012, 2015, 2019, 2021, 2023
FIFA World Cup Golden Ball (Best player of tournament)	2	2014, 2022
Argentina Player of the Year	14	2005, 2007-2013, 2015-2017, 2019-2021
La Liga Player of the Year	6	2008/09, 2009/10, 2010/11, 2011/12, 2012/13, 2014/15
La Liga top scorer (Pichichi trophy)	8	2009/10, 2011/12, 2012/13, 2016/17, 2017/18, 2018/19, 2019/20, 2020/21
European Golden Boot (Top scorer across Europe)	6	2009/10, 2011/12, 2012/13, 2016/17, 2017/18, 2018/19
FIFA World Player of the Year (Awarded from 1991-2015)	1	2009
FIFA The Best Award (Player of the Year est. 2015)	2	2019, 2022
FIFA Club World Cup Golden Ball	2	2009, 2011

Award   Titles Year/Season

Pelé, Maradona, and Messi's Stats

	Messi	Pelé	Maradona
Club games in domestic league play	616	647	491
Club Goals	508	606	259
Domestic League Titles	10	7	3
International Club Titles	7	4	1
Senior International Games	178	92	91
Senior *International Goals*	106	77	34
Continental Titles	1	0	0
World Cup Titles	1	3	1

MESSI: THE UNMATCHED PHENOMENON

Lionel Messi stands as an unparalleled force in the realm of football, his prowess on the field leaving an indelible mark on the sport's history. The weight of his achievements is further magnified when we delve into the annals of time, where his unparalleled talent and unrivalled records become evident. By delving into history, we not only gain a profound understanding of Messi's extraordinary abilities but also glean invaluable lessons from the triumphs and failures of the past. Armed with this knowledge, we can fortify ourselves for the challenges that lie ahead, ensuring a more enlightened and resolute approach to the future.

By the time Messi reached the tender age of 20, his exceptional talent had already propelled him to the pinnacle of global football stardom. Revered icons of the game such as

Diego Maradona and Ronaldinho, renowned for their own extraordinary skills, unequivocally anointed Messi as the supreme player in the world. Ronaldinho, a maestro in his own right, humbly admitted that he paled in comparison to Messi's brilliance, boldly declaring that he was not even the finest player in their shared team of Barcelona. Such an admission served as a resounding testament to Messi's unparalleled prowess and cemented his status as a true footballing prodigy.

Four years after Lionel Messi's historic victory in winning his first Ballon d'Or, a fervent public debate was ignited, centered around the extraordinary qualities that elevated him beyond the realm of contemporary footballers. People were captivated by Messi's unrivaled prowess on the field, contemplating the notion that he might just be the greatest player in the world. Adding fuel to this discussion was the unwavering endorsement of Messi's former manager, the esteemed Pep Guardiola, who boldly declared Messi as the finest player he had ever coached. This proclamation was ultimately validated by Barcelona's triumphant treble victories in the ensuing years.

As time progressed, Messi's game transcended boundaries, effortlessly conquering various playing styles and garnering immense admiration from all corners of Europe. The comparisons between Messi and football legends Diego Maradona and Pelé became inevitable, with many Europeans daring to place Messi above these iconic figures. Even Maradona himself, a football deity in his own right, acknowledged Messi's unparalleled talent, proclaiming that he had never witnessed a player more deserving of inheriting his position on the Argentine national team.

In the grand tapestry of football history, Messi's impact and legacy continued to grow, solidifying his status as a true legend of the sport. His remarkable abilities, combined with his insatiable hunger for success, propelled him to heights previously unimaginable. Thus, the public debate surrounding Messi's greatness served as a testament to his exceptional skills, leaving no doubt that he had transcended the boundaries of football to become a transcendent force in the world of sports.

Throughout his illustrious career, Lionel Messi has been constantly compared to the legendary Diego

Maradona by his fellow Argentines. This comparison stems from their strikingly similar playing styles as diminutive, left-footed dribblers. Initially, Messi was seen as just another talented Argentine player, joining the likes of his childhood idol Pablo Aimar, to receive the prestigious title of the "NEW MARADONA." However, as Messi's career progressed, he not only lived up to this moniker but surpassed all previous contenders, solidifying himself as one of the greatest players Argentina has ever produced since Maradona.

Jorge Valdano, who had the privilege of winning the 1986 World Cup alongside Maradona, showered Messi with praise in October 2013, stating, "Messi is Maradona every day. For the past five years, Messi has been the Maradona of the World Cup in Mexico." Cesar Menotti echoed this sentiment, acknowledging that Messi plays "at the level of the best Maradona." These esteemed individuals, along with numerous other notable Argentines, firmly believe that Messi has surpassed Maradona as the greatest player in the history of football.

Despite the overwhelming admiration and accolades, there remains a faction in Argentina that places Messi below Maradona within the context of Argentine society. This perspective stems not only from Messi's less-than-average performance for the Argentine National Team but also from the perceived differences between the two men in terms of class, personality, and background. However, it is important to note that such comparisons are subjective and do not diminish the undeniable talent and achievements of Messi, who has consistently dazzled the world with his exceptional skills and records.

Throughout history, Lionel Messi has shattered an astounding number of records, cementing his status as a legendary figure in the world of football. Not only has he established numerous records, but he has also pushed the boundaries of what was once thought possible, leaving a lasting impact on the sport. While it is customary to view records as achievements waiting to be surpassed, conquering certain milestones can be an arduous feat that requires unparalleled dedication and skill. Unlike many other players, Messi, aptly nicknamed "no-mercy-against-opponents," possesses the audacity and talent to breach longstanding gaps that have stood unchallenged for ages, highlighting his relentless pursuit of greatness.

While engaging in discussions about players from different eras can be an intriguing exercise, it is undeniably more enlightening to evaluate Lionel Messi alongside his contemporaries. What sets Messi apart is his distinctive playing style, which initially appears amiable but swiftly transforms into an unforgiving force once he scores against his opponents. It is often a common tendency for individuals to compare Messi and Ronaldo due to their extensive time spent playing together. However, what many fail to grasp is that Messi and Ronaldo possess contrasting approaches to the game. One exudes a level of aggression that surpasses the other, and this divergence is only natural as our temperaments can never be identical. Messi's game play is adorned with an abundance of extraordinary features that elevate him to a league of his own as a playmaker-forward. The sheer magnitude of his incomparability is such that it invites debates and discussions about his greatness. Yet, it is undeniable that consistently wielding his mastery as a game-changer on the field is a testament to his greatness. While some may label his dominance in the football realm as "controversial," Messi's unwavering presence in the power struggle is a testament to his exceptional abilities. This essay has already delved into his awe-inspiring goal scoring, mesmerizing dribbling skills, and unparalleled game understanding. However, the argument remains to be made and demonstrated that Messi is indeed the epitome of professional football's finest player.

As previously mentioned, Arsene Wenger, the manager of Arsenal FC, unequivocally declared Lionel Messi as both the best player in the world and the greatest player of all time. This sentiment is shared by numerous football legends, who believe that Messi's unparalleled natural ability is unlikely to be matched by anyone else. What is truly astonishing is that despite already achieving such greatness, we still anticipate extraordinary performances from Messi. At the age of 28, he has the potential to showcase his incomparable talent for many more years, ensuring that his greatness will surpass the boundaries of time and different eras in football.

HEAD-TO-HEAD: MESSI VS PELE

As reiterated earlier, Arsene Wenger, the esteemed manager of Arsenal FC, has made a resolute declaration that leaves no room for doubt: Lionel Messi is not only the finest player in the world but also the greatest player to have ever graced the sport. This sentiment is not confined to Wenger alone; it resonates with numerous revered football legends who firmly believe that Messi's exceptional natural abilities are unparalleled and highly unlikely to be replicated by any other player. What truly astounds us is that despite having already achieved such unparalleled greatness, we continue to eagerly anticipate extraordinary performances from Messi. At the relatively young age of 28, he possesses the potential to exhibit his incomparable talent for many more years to come, ensuring that his greatness transcends the constraints of time and different eras in football.

The legendary footballer, Edison Arantes do Nascimento, universally known as Pelé, left an indelible mark on the sport. Born on October 21st, 1940, in Brazil, Pelé's extraordinary talent and unparalleled goal-scoring prowess propelled him to greatness. Throughout his illustrious career, he etched his name in the annals of football history by netting a staggering 1,281 goals in 1,363 games. These goals encompassed not only official matches but also unofficial friendly and tour games, sparking controversy among sports enthusiasts who marvelled at his seemingly insurmountable feat. However, the veil of scepticism was lifted when it was unveiled that Pelé's remarkable tally encompassed goals from all types of matches. This revelation solidified his position in the Guinness Book of World Records as the football player with the highest number of goals scored during his awe-inspiring career. Pelé's extraordinary achievements continue to inspire generations of footballers and cement his status as an immortal icon of the beautiful game.

Pelé's impact on society extended far beyond the football field. Recognized as a man with a strong social conscience, he tirelessly advocated for policies to uplift the impoverished communities in Brazil. While some may hesitate to label him an activist, his unwavering support for social improvement cannot be denied. In fact, his contributions were so significant that Brazilian President Janio Quadros bestowed upon him the prestigious title of national treasure in 1961, a testament to his immense influence and revered status.

One remarkable incident stands out in Pelé's illustrious career, highlighting his ability to transcend the boundaries of sports and bring people together. During the tumultuous Biafra War in Nigeria, Pelé's mere presence had such a profound impact that a two-day cease-fire was declared. This unprecedented pause in the conflict allowed the war-stricken population to bask in the joy of witnessing the unrivaled skills of "The King" of the Beautiful Game. It is a testament to Pelé's unparalleled charisma and universal appeal that he could halt the ravages of war, if only temporarily, through the power of his talent and personality.

Renowned Uruguayan writer Eduardo Galeano perfectly captures the essence of Pelé's football style in his seminal work, "Soccer in Sun and Shadow." Galeano's words beautifully encapsulate the magic and artistry that Pelé brought to the game, transcending mere athleticism.

Pelé's grace, finesse, and unparalleled skill on the field mesmerized audiences worldwide, leaving an indelible mark on the history of football.

In conclusion, Pelé's impact extended far beyond his football achievements. He used his platform to advocate for social change, earning the admiration and recognition of both his fellow countrymen and world leaders. His ability to unite people and inspire cease-fires during times of conflict showcases the extraordinary power he held over the hearts and minds of individuals. Pelé's football style, eloquently described by Galeano, will forever be remembered as a testament to his unparalleled talent and the beauty he brought to the game.

Furthermore, Galeano eloquently emphasizes that those fortunate enough to witness his brilliance on the field were bestowed with a profound gift of unparalleled splendour. These fleeting instances were so profoundly captivating, so incredibly awe-inspiring, that they instilled within us an unwavering belief in the existence of immortality itself.

Messi's exceptional career goal-scoring prowess has drawn comparisons to the legendary Pelé. With a staggering 1,280 goals to his name, Pelé's record remains unmatched, while Messi has already amassed an impressive 821 goals and continues to add to his tally.

The two football icons have also been evaluated in terms of their league title triumphs. Messi, a force to be reckoned with, has claimed an astounding six league titles, accompanied by three continental championships. In comparison, Pelé's illustrious career saw him secure an impressive seven league titles and two continental championships.

These remarkable achievements further solidify Messi and Pelé's status as football legends, constantly pushing the boundaries of the sport and etching their names in the annals of history.

Pelé, a legendary figure in the world of football, is forever associated with the 1958 World Cup, where his remarkable talent shone through at the tender age of 17. Scoring twice in the finals, he left an indelible mark on the tournament. Pelé's magic continued to captivate audiences in the 1962 and 1970 World Cups, where he once again found the back of the net in the finals.

In contrast, Lionel Messi, a prodigious talent in both the Argentine and European leagues, has faced disappointment on the grandest stage of them all - the World Cup. The Brazil 2014 Finals saw Argentina succumb to Germany, leaving Messi's dream of a World Cup victory unfulfilled. For years, the elusive World Cup seemed like the missing piece in Messi's illustrious career, casting a shadow over his otherwise glittering trophy cabinet.

However, destiny had other plans for Messi. In a moment of sheer triumph, Argentina emerged victorious over France in the 2022 World Cup, finally securing the coveted title. This triumph not only brought joy to the nation but also marked a personal triumph for Messi, as he now held both the World Cup and Copa America, the two most significant international trophies for a South American player.

With this historic achievement, Messi has solidified his status as one of the greatest footballers of all time, joining the ranks of Pelé and other legendary figures. The long and arduous journey has finally culminated in a glorious triumph, forever etching Messi's name in the annals of football history.

The rivalry between Messi and Pelé is fueled by their respective fan bases, who passionately argue for their chosen player as the best in the world. Some fans believe that Messi's skills and achievements make him the greatest, while others argue that Pelé's accomplishments and longevity in the sport make him the superior player.

In one quote, Pelé expressed his admiration for Messi and stated that he would love to play alongside him. However, he also criticized Messi for his perceived weakness in using his head during gameplay. Pelé's comment suggests that he believes Messi lacks a certain aspect of the game that he himself possessed.

On another occasion, Pelé highlighted his own achievement of scoring 1,000 goals and implied that Messi cannot be considered a legend unless he reaches that milestone. This statement implies that Pelé views his own goal-scoring record as a defining factor in determining a player's status as a legend.

The intense rivalry between Messi and Pelé, as well as the contrasting opinions of their fan bases, contribute to the ongoing debate about who is the greatest player of all time. Ultimately, the comparison between these two football legends is subjective and depends on individual preferences and criteria for greatness.

The ongoing debate comparing the statistical prowess of Messi and Pelé seems endless. However, distinguished experts have succinctly differentiated these two legends, providing us with valuable guidance. According to their analysis, Messi excels in close control, surpassing Pelé in the art of dribbling. On the other hand, Pelé's strength lies in his ability to make precise passes, showcasing his exceptional team-playing skills. While Pelé strategically utilizes his team, making him an outstanding team player, Messi's style leans more towards being a flashy player, combining his dribbling skills with his playmaking abilities.

HEAD-TO-HEAD: MESSI VS MARADONA

Messi and Maradona possess remarkably similar qualities as football players, yet their individual career paths distinguish them as truly exceptional. Initially regarded as Maradona's heir apparent, Messi surpassed expectations by transcending the role of a mere successor to become an extraordinary force in his own right. For years, the World Cup title eluded Messi, leaving a void in his impressive collection of accolades. However, Argentina's triumphant victory over France in the 2022 World Cup marked a pivotal moment, as Messi secured the two most coveted international trophies for a South American player - the World Cup and the Copa America. This achievement solidifies Messi's legacy as a truly iconic figure in the realm of football.

To truly grasp the depth of the Messi-Maradona comparison, it is imperative that we lend an ear to the perspectives of others. Adeline succinctly sums it up by stating, "Messi is in a league of his own, distinct from Maradona—this viewpoint is crucial in assessing Messi's abilities." The conclusion of the World Cup serves as a pivotal moment for evaluating football players, including the likes of C lo, Kaka, and of course, Messi. The defeat suffered by Argentina serves as a valuable lesson, prompting them to reevaluate their coach Maradona and seek new leadership for their team. This transformative step will allow Argentina to redefine their image, moving away from the era of Maradona and towards a brighter future.

Once again, during an appearance on a prominent television program called "Monday on America," Palermo made a bold declaration about Messi, emphasizing that he believes Messi falls short of being comparable to the legendary Maradona. Palermo firmly asserted that Messi lacks the same indomitable mindset and determination that Maradona possessed. In Palermo's perspective, Messi simply lacks the necessary readiness and resilience to shoulder the weight of responsibility that Maradona effortlessly carried throughout his career.

Through extensive interviews with players, coaches, and commentators, it has been unequivocally established that Messi stands as the unrivalled epitome of football excellence on a global scale. However, it is important to acknowledge that this assertion is not without its share of controversy, as there are dissenting voices who refuse to acknowledge his unparalleled brilliance. Nevertheless, what is truly astonishing is that amidst such differing opinions, one cannot ignore the overwhelming consensus among these individuals who unanimously express their astonishment at the sheer magnitude of Messi's extraordinary abilities.

Regarding this matter, a trusted assistant to the legendary Messi expressed his perspective with conviction, stating, "I have always regarded him as an exceptional individual, but it seems rather inappropriate to criticize a talented 23-year-old for not shouldering the burden of an entire team and holding his youthful accomplishments against him. Perhaps the focus should be on the 36-year-old, who possesses a mere 15 international appearances and a mere 13 minutes of playtime in the World Cup. It would have been more appropriate for him to either have achieved more himself or refrained from making such comments."

It is important to remember that during Maradona's time, Barcelona FC was not the dominant force it is today. The team was considerably weaker in the early 1980s, failing to bring home trophies for Diego as they have done since Messi's arrival. When Maradona departed Barcelona in 1984 after a two-year stint, the Catalans had not won the league championship in the previous ten years. In stark contrast, Maradona played a pivotal role in Napoli's success during the same decade, leading them to two Serie A titles and two runner-up positions in just four seasons. These two league titles remain the only championships Napoli has ever won in their history. Additionally, let's not forget Maradona's remarkable achievement of winning the 1986 World Cup with Argentina.

When analysing Messi's exceptional performances in European games and comparing them to Maradona's, it becomes evident that Messi has not only lived up to his role-model's legacy but has even surpassed it. The sheer brilliance displayed by Messi on the field has proven him to be a force to be reckoned with, leaving no doubt that he has outshined his idol in terms of skill, technique, and overall impact on the game.

MESSI VERSUS MARADONA: BREAKDOWN OF THEIR GOALS IN EUROPE		
	MESSI	**MARADONA**
GAMES	482	346
GOALS	412	161
GOALS IN FINALS	20	3
PENALTIES	49	47
FREE-KICK GOALS	16	32
GOALS AFTER RECEIVING BALL OUTSIDE BOX	141	47
OPEN PLAY GOALS	347	82
GOALS AFTER 1+ DRIBBLES	99	22
GOALS AFTER 2+ DRIBBLES	31	3
GOALS AFTER 3+ DRIBBLES	15	2
GOALS AFTER 4+ DRIBBLES	5	0

Messi's dominance in terms of numbers has always set him apart from Maradona, but the absence of a World Cup victory has cast a shadow over his legacy for Argentina. However, with the prestigious World Cup trophy now in his possession, Messi has finally filled that void. Let's delve into the detailed statistics of both players for their national team, without drawing any definitive conclusions.

In terms of overall appearances, Messi has taken the field for Argentina a staggering 172 times, while Maradona's presence stands at 91 matches. When it comes to the grand stage of the World Cup, Maradona has graced the tournament with his skills in 21 games, whereas Messi has surpassed him with 26 appearances. This achievement also saw Messi surpass the legendary Lothar Matthaus, who previously held the record for the most World Cup matches played with 25.

Furthermore, in the realm of World Cup goals, Messi's tally stands at an impressive 13, surpassing Maradona's record of eight goals. However, it is worth noting that Maradona's impact in the World Cup cannot be undermined, as his goals were instrumental in securing Argentina's victory in the tournament during his era.

Looking beyond the World Cup, Maradona's overall goal count for Argentina reaches 34, showcasing his prowess as a prolific scorer. In contrast, Messi has found the back of the net an astounding 97 times, highlighting his incredible goal-scoring ability and consistent contributions to the national team.

These statistics shed light on the remarkable careers of both Messi and Maradona, each leaving their own indelible mark on the Argentine national team. While Messi's numbers may surpass Maradona's in certain aspects, the legacy and impact of both players cannot be simply measured by figures alone.

THE BATTLE OF MESSI AND RONALDO

These two extraordinary players stand out for their exceptional achievements, each achieving success in their own distinctive way. However, it is unnecessary to dwell on words when the latest statistics can eloquently convey their prowess: Messi has remarkably netted 821 goals in 1047 appearances for both his club and country, while Ronaldo has astonishingly scored 873 goals in 1204 appearances. To delve deeper into their remarkable performances, let us turn our attention to the table below, which provides a comprehensive comparison of Messi's and Ronaldo's accomplishments during the 2015/2016 season.

The intensity of the rivalry between Messi and Ronaldo reached unprecedented heights due to their astonishing goalscoring abilities. Both players consistently averaged more than one goal per game during their peak years, which was truly remarkable. Throughout Ronaldo's nine-year tenure at Real Madrid, both Messi and Ronaldo scored a goal every 85 minutes in all competitions, matching each other blow for blow. Their adjacency in goalscoring has been nothing short of astounding over the years.

Goals Scoring

When we examine their entire careers, Messi slightly edges out Ronaldo with a ratio of 0.78 goals per game compared to Ronaldo's 0.73 goals per game. If we delve deeper into goals per minutes, Messi scores a goal every 105 minutes, while Ronaldo scores a goal every 112 minutes. However, it's worth noting that Ronaldo has more career goals than Messi, with 873 goals compared to Messi's 821 goals. This difference can be attributed to Ronaldo playing 157 more games than Messi throughout his career.

Despite Messi having a slight advantage in the overall ratio, it's important to consider the differing paths they took early in their careers. Ronaldo spent more of his formative years as a traditional right winger before fully embracing goalscoring as his primary role in 2006, three to four years into his career. On the other hand, Messi took two to three years to transform from a speedy winger into a player with an insatiable hunger for goals. Taking these distinct beginnings into account, the ratios between them would be even closer.

When comparing Messi and Ronaldo, it becomes evident that goalscoring is the most challenging aspect to differentiate them on. Both players have left an indelible mark on the football world with their extraordinary ability to find the back of the net.

Assisting

Lionel Messi reigns supreme in the realm of assists, standing shoulder to shoulder with the most exceptional playmakers in history, and his staggering numbers leave no room for doubt. Throughout his illustrious career, Messi has amassed a remarkable total of 361 assists in 1047 appearances, in stark contrast to Ronaldo's commendable 249 assists achieved in 1204 games. Nevertheless, it is crucial not to fall into the trap of undervaluing Ronaldo's prowess in this domain simply because Messi holds a clear advantage. Ronaldo's assist count remains astonishing when compared to the mere mortals who grace the beautiful game. In fact, Ronaldo boasts an even greater number of assists in the prestigious Champions League, with an impressive tally of 41 compared to Messi's 40 assists. Admittedly, Ronaldo has participated in 20 more matches than Messi, but this fact does not diminish the significance of his achievement. However, it would be remiss to disregard Messi's overall assist statistics, which undeniably solidify his status as a true maestro.

Passing

When it comes to passing, Lionel Messi emerges as the undeniable champion in this category, as evidenced by his impressive stats. However, it is crucial to acknowledge that Ronaldo's passing abilities are often underrated. Looking at their performances in the league and Champions League since 2009/10, Messi has made a remarkable 1393 key passes in 599 appearances, while Ronaldo has managed to deliver 933 key passes in 561 appearances. Moreover, Messi's dominance extends to the through ball statistics, with an astonishing 450 successful through balls during the same period, compared to Ronaldo's 81 successful through balls. Undoubtedly, Messi's passing numbers are significantly superior, but it is important to note that Ronaldo's achievements in this aspect are still remarkable. Furthermore, it is reasonable to assume that Ronaldo's passing stats would have been even higher before 2009, when he played a more involved role in the creative build-up play.

Dribbling

Ronaldo embarked on his football journey as a crafty winger, relying on his lightning-fast speed and exceptional skill to outmaneuver and outwit defenders. However, as his career progressed, he underwent a transformation, taking on the roles of an inside-forward and striker. Consequently, his reliance on dribbling has diminished significantly in his performances.

In contrast, Messi's early days in the sport saw him primarily stationed on the sidelines, but he eventually shifted to a more central position, becoming the linchpin of his team. Yet, Messi's style of play deviates greatly from that of a traditional center-forward, as his innate talents as a Number 10 player make him the epitome of a False

9. This unique role sees him drop deeper into the field, actively involving himself in the play rather than solely relying on runs and exploiting defenders' weaknesses.

Due to his tendency to retreat towards the heart of the action, Messi continues to incorporate dribbling as a crucial aspect of his game. Astonishingly, he has completed an astounding 3094 successful dribbles in both league and Champions League matches since 2003/04. In comparison, Ronaldo has accumulated 1680 successful dribbles over the same period. These statistics undeniably highlight Messi's unparalleled prowess in the art of dribbling.

Therefore, it is indisputable that Lionel Messi reigns supreme when it comes to showcasing exceptional dribbling abilities on the football field.

Headings

There is no denying that heading is an area where Ronaldo shines brightly, leaving Messi in his shadow. Throughout their illustrious careers, Ronaldo has displayed an unparalleled prowess in heading, scoring a staggering 147 goals from headers in 1204 appearances. In stark contrast, Messi has managed to find the back of the net with his head on only 26 occasions in 1047 appearances.

But Ronaldo's dominance in heading doesn't stop there. Not only has he excelled in scoring headed goals, but he has also emerged victorious in a remarkable 771 aerial duels in both domestic leagues and the prestigious Champions League since the 2009/10 season. In comparison, Messi has won a modest 116 aerial duels.

It is hardly surprising that these numbers heavily favor Ronaldo when we consider their contrasting physical attributes, playing styles, and the tactics employed by their respective teams. Ronaldo's towering presence coupled with his remarkable leaping ability and timing make him a force to be reckoned with in the air. On the other hand, Messi's smaller stature and preference for dribbling and intricate footwork naturally limit his impact in aerial battles.

In conclusion, the statistics unequivocally highlight Ronaldo's dominance in the art of heading, solidifying his reputation as one of the greatest aerial threats in the history of the game.

Shooting

When it comes to shooting, the numbers speak for themselves: Ronaldo has consistently outperformed Messi in terms of shot volume. Since the 2009/10 season, Ronaldo has unleashed a staggering 3644 shots in both league and Champions League matches, compared to Messi's 2941 shots. This demonstrates Ronaldo's relentless drive to find the back of the net.

However, it's not just about the quantity of shots, but also the quality. Messi's precision and accuracy are truly remarkable. He converts a higher percentage of his shots, finding the back of the net with every 5.27 attempts, while Ronaldo does so with every 6.43 shots. This showcases Messi's exceptional ability to make the most of his opportunities.

Moreover, Messi's accuracy is further highlighted by his ability to hit the target. He gets an impressive 47.19% of his shots on target, whereas Ronaldo manages 41.16%.

This indicates Messi's superior ability to consistently trouble opposing goalkeepers.

Despite Messi's efficiency, Ronaldo's sheer volume of attempts cannot be ignored. The fact that he can generate such a large number of shots is a testament to his relentless attacking mindset and his ability to create scoring opportunities for himself.

Furthermore, Ronaldo possesses an edge in certain areas. He excels at shooting from long-range, showcasing his ability to score from distance. Additionally, Ronaldo's proficiency with both his weak foot and his head sets him apart. These skills make him a formidable threat from any angle or situation.

Considering all these factors, it is difficult to declare a clear winner between Ronaldo and Messi in terms of shooting prowess. While Messi's efficiency and accuracy are exceptional, Ronaldo's ability to produce a high volume of attempts, combined with his proficiency in various shooting techniques, makes this battle too close to call. Both players possess unique strengths that make them exceptional.

Penalty kick

Contrary to popular belief, Ronaldo's penalty record surpasses Messi's, although not by as wide a margin as some may think. While the media often portrays Messi as unreliable from the spot, labeling Ronaldo as the ultimate penalty king, the reality lies somewhere in between. Excluding shootouts, Ronaldo has remarkably scored 161 penalties throughout his illustrious career, albeit with 29 misses. On the other hand, Messi has netted 108 penalties, but with 31 unfortunate misses. Consequently, Ronaldo boasts an impressive overall penalty conversion rate of 85%, while Messi stands at 78%. Undeniably, Ronaldo's statistics outshine Messi's, yet he falls short of being as dependable as he is often depicted. Other elite strikers such as Lewandowski and Ibrahimovic boast significantly higher conversion rates. When it comes to significant penalty misses, Messi faltered in the 2016 Copa America final shootout against Chile and the 2012 Champions League semi-final against Chelsea. As for Ronaldo, his most notable penalty blunders occurred in the 2008 Champions League final shootout against

Chelsea, where his Manchester United team ultimately triumphed due to John Terry's miss, and in the 2012 Champions League semi-final shootout against Bayern Munich, which proved fatal for Real Madrid.

Free Kick

In recent years, Lionel Messi has undeniably emerged as the ultimate free kick specialist, showcasing his exceptional skills in this aspect of the game. On the other hand, Cristiano Ronaldo's proficiency in free kicks has experienced a somewhat alarming decline. However, it would be an oversimplification to label this category as straightforward, as it overlooks the influence of recency bias.

Examining the statistics, it is true that from 2017 to 2019, Messi outshined Ronaldo by scoring an impressive 23 free kick goals compared to Ronaldo's modest 5. Nevertheless, delving further into the past reveals a different narrative. In the period from 2009 to 2011, Ronaldo showcased his prowess by netting an astonishing 21 direct free kick goals, while Messi managed only 3. These figures highlight the dynamic nature of their performances over time.

When considering the all-time career stats, Messi has now amassed a remarkable tally of 65 free kick goals, surpassing Ronaldo's 61. This achievement is even more remarkable considering that just a few years ago, the free kick category seemed like a sure win for Cristiano Ronaldo. However, Messi's stunning turnaround in recent years has not only allowed him to catch up with Ronaldo but has also given him the edge with a superior free kick conversion rate. Thus, it can be argued that Messi slightly edges out Ronaldo in this aspect of the game.

Hat Tricks

The goal-scoring prowess of Messi and Ronaldo is simply mind-blowing, as evidenced by their jaw-dropping combined total of 120 hat tricks. Messi boasts an impressive record of 57 career hat tricks, while Ronaldo trails just behind with an astonishing 63. Although Ronaldo may hold the overall lead, Messi edges him out in terms of frequency, scoring a hat trick every 18.4 games compared to Ronaldo's 19.1 games. These figures are incredibly close, highlighting the extraordinary talent possessed by both players.

Not only do Messi and Ronaldo excel in overall hat trick counts, but their performances in league games and the prestigious Champions League are equally remarkable. In league matches, Messi has notched an outstanding 36 hat tricks, while Ronaldo has an astounding 42 to his name. This demonstrates their consistent ability to dominate their respective leagues and leave their opponents in awe.

Even in the fiercely competitive Champions League, where the best of the best clash, Messi and Ronaldo have managed to achieve an extraordinary feat. Both superstars have scored an impressive eight hat tricks each, showcasing their unrivaled ability to rise to the occasion and deliver exceptional performances on the grandest stage.

The numbers speak for themselves, painting a picture of two footballing legends who continually push the boundaries of what is deemed possible. Messi and Ronaldo's relentless pursuit of excellence has catapulted them into a realm of greatness rarely witnessed in the history of the sport. Their incredible goal-scoring records and unwavering hunger for success solidify their status as the epitome of footballing brilliance.

Individual Awards

No other footballers in the entire history of the sport have been able to maintain such an extraordinary level of skill and performance for such an extended period as Lionel Messi and Cristiano Ronaldo. Their dominance over the prestigious Ballon d'Or award has been relentless, with Messi's collection of 8 Ballon d'Or trophies slightly surpassing Ronaldo's impressive haul of 5. It is worth noting that no other player in the history of football has managed to win more than 3 of these coveted awards.

If Messi and Ronaldo had not been competing against each other for the Ballon d'Or over the years, it is not at all inconceivable that one of them could have easily secured the award a staggering 10 times or even more. Their exceptional talents and unrivaled performances have set them apart from the rest of the footballing world.

When it comes to UEFA's top accolades, Ronaldo takes the lead with an impressive tally of 4 awards, including the UEFA Club Footballer of the Year, UEFA Best Player in Europe (twice), and UEFA Men's Player of the Year. Messi, on the other hand, has secured 3 of these prestigious honors, including the UEFA Club Footballer of the Year and UEFA Best Player in Europe (twice). Their contributions to the European footballing scene have been nothing short of remarkable.

In terms of individual scoring prowess, Messi has clinched the title of the league's top scorer on an astonishing 8 occasions, resulting in him winning the European Golden Shoe an impressive 6 times. Ronaldo, not to be outdone, has finished as the league's top scorer 5 times, with his achievements spanning across different leagues such as the Premier League, Serie A, and La Liga. This remarkable feat has earned him 4 European Golden Shoes, solidifying his status as one of the greatest goal scorers in history.

While Ronaldo has been honored with the prestigious Puskas award for the best goal in a calendar year, receiving 2 nominations, Messi has surprisingly missed out on this accolade despite being nominated an incredible 7 times. However, Messi has claimed the Golden Ball, which is awarded to the best player of the tournament at the World Cup, on two occasions. His exceptional performances led his team to the final in 2014 and secured victory in 2022. Additionally, he has been crowned Copa America's Best Player twice and has also been recognized as the Best Young Player once.

The enduring excellence displayed by Messi and Ronaldo throughout their careers is unparalleled in the history of football. Their numerous accolades, awards, and records serve as a testament to their indomitable talent, skill, and dedication to the beautiful game.

Trophies

In terms of accolades and achievements, Lionel Messi holds the upper hand, having secured a remarkable 44 trophies compared to Cristiano Ronaldo's 35 trophies. It is worth noting that Messi's tally includes his triumph at the 2008 Olympic Games and the 2005 U-20 World Cup. On the international stage, Messi has now triumphed in both the Copa America and the World Cup with Argentina, while Ronaldo has claimed victory in the Euros with Portugal and lifted the Nations League trophy. Additionally, Messi boasts an impressive 12 league titles, overshadowing Ronaldo's 7. However, when it comes to Champions League glory, Ronaldo has the advantage, having secured the prestigious title 5 times, while Messi has achieved it 4 times. Although the margin is slim, when considering the overall numbers, Messi currently holds a slight edge over Ronaldo.

Records

In summary, both Messi and Ronaldo have an impressive array of records to their names. One of the most remarkable achievements is Messi's Guinness World Record for scoring an astounding 91 goals in a single calendar year in 2012. To put this into perspective, Messi's closest rival is himself with 60 goals, while Ronaldo's personal best stands at 69. Scoring 91 goals in a year is truly out of this world.

However, when it comes to the Champions League, Ronaldo reigns supreme in the record books. He holds the records for the most goals, most assists, most free kick goals, most hat-tricks (shared with Messi), and most goals in a single season. On the other hand, Messi has numerous European records at the domestic level, including the most league goals scored in a single season

(50 goals) and the most consecutive league matches scored in worldwide (21 matches, 33 goals).

In terms of international achievements, Ronaldo takes the crown as the all-time top scorer with an unbelievable 128 goals. Meanwhile, Messi holds the title for the highest scoring South American player of all time with 106 goals. These accomplishments highlight the incredible talent and impact both players have had on the world of football.

International Achievements

Both Cristiano Ronaldo and Lionel Messi have enjoyed remarkable careers at the international level, showcasing their extraordinary talent. While their statistics for their national teams may not be as mind-boggling as their club performances, they are still incredibly impressive. Ronaldo has an astonishing goal-scoring rate of one goal every 127 minutes for Portugal, while Messi follows closely behind with a goal every 141 minutes for Argentina. When considering their contributions through assists as well, Ronaldo makes a goal contribution every 100 minutes, while Messi does so every 94 minutes.

Ronaldo holds the prestigious title of Portugal's all-time top scorer, netting an impressive 128 goals in just 205 appearances. On the other hand, Messi proudly stands as Argentina's all-time leading goal scorer, with an outstanding tally of 106 goals in 180 appearances. These records speak volumes about their immense impact on their respective national teams.

In terms of individual accolades, Ronaldo has claimed the Euro 2021 Golden Boot, awarded to the top scorer of the tournament, as well as the Silver Boot during Euro 2016 for scoring the second most goals. Meanwhile, Messi has achieved extraordinary success, becoming the only player in history to win the World Cup Golden Ball twice, in 2014 and 2022. He has also clinched the Copa America Golden Ball twice, in 2015 and 2021, recognizing him as the best player of those tournaments. Adding to his impressive collection, Messi secured the Golden Boot at Copa America 2021 and the Silver Boot at the 2022 World Cup.

These accomplishments highlight the exceptional abilities and impact of both Ronaldo and Messi on the international stage, solidifying their positions as two of the greatest footballers of all time.

Messi's journey at the international level has been filled with heartbreak, having lost in four major finals. However, his perseverance paid off when he finally achieved triumph with his country at the Copa America 2021, marking a historic moment for him. But his success didn't stop there. In 2022, Messi showcased his exceptional skills by leading his team to victory in the Finalissima trophy, a monumental clash between UEFA and CONMEBOL champions, where they defeated the formidable European champions, Italy.

But Messi's hunger for success didn't end there. Later that year, he reached the pinnacle of football glory by lifting the World Cup, cementing his status as one of the greatest players of all time. These remarkable achievements are further enhanced by his previous accomplishments, including an Olympic Gold medal with the Argentina U23 side and the FIFA U20 World Cup trophy.

On the other hand, Ronaldo, with the Portuguese national team, has also tasted the sweetness of victory on the international stage. He reached two major finals, emerging victorious in the 2016 European Championships and narrowly missing out on the title in Euro 2004. Additionally, Ronaldo's leadership guided Portugal to triumph in the UEFA Nations League. Notably, he holds the record for the most goals in the history of international football, a testament to his incredible goal-scoring prowess.

While Ronaldo may have the edge in terms of goal-scoring records, Messi shines brighter when it comes to individual accolades. With an unprecedented four Best Player awards at major tournaments, he has etched his name in history as the most decorated player in this regard. And now, with his recent victories in both the Copa America and the World Cup, Messi has solidified his legacy as a true champion.

In conclusion, Messi's journey has been marked by heartache, triumph, and an impressive collection of individual honors. His recent conquests at the Copa

America and the World Cup have elevated him to legendary status, while Ronaldo's achievements cannot be undermined, particularly his goal-scoring prowess and success in major tournaments. Ultimately, the debate between these two football icons will continue, but Messi's recent accomplishments have undeniably left an indelible mark on the history of the sport.

International Tournament Awards and Achievements

Lionel Messi	Cristiano Ronaldo

Lionel Messi	Cristiano Ronaldo
<ul><li>2022 World Cup Winner</li><li>2022 Finalissima Winner</li><li>2021 Copa America Winner</li><li>2008 Olympics Gold Medal</li><li>2005 FIFA U20 World Cup Winner</li></ul><ul><li>2016 Copa America Runner-up</li><li>2015 Copa America Runner-up</li><li>2014 FIFA World Cup Runner-up</li><li>2007 Copa America Runner-up</li></ul><ul><li>2022 World Cup Golden Ball</li><li>2022 Finalissima Best Player</li><li>2021 Copa America Golden Ball</li><li>2015 Copa America Golden Ball</li><li>2014 World Cup Golden Ball</li><li>2007 Copa America Best Young Player</li><li>2005 U20 World Cup Golden Ball</li></ul><ul><li>2022 World Cup Silver Boot</li><li>2021 Copa America Golden Boot</li><li>2016 Copa America 2nd Top Scorer</li><li>2005 U20 World Cup Golden Boot</li></ul><ul><li>2022 World Cup Top Assister (5 players on 3)</li><li>2021 Copa America Top Assister</li><li>2018 World Cup Top</li></ul>	<ul><li>2016 Euros Winner</li><li>2019 Nations League Winner</li></ul><ul><li>2004 Euros Runner-up</li></ul><ul><li>2021 Euros Golden Boot</li><li>2019 Nations League Finals Golden Boot</li><li>2016 Euros Silver Boot</li><li>Euro 2012 joint top scorer (6 players on 3 - Torres Golden Boot)</li></ul><ul><li>2019 Nations League Finals Goal of the Tournament</li></ul>

Lionel Messi	Cristiano Ronaldo
Assister (16 players on 2) • 2016 Copa America Top Assister • 2015 Copa America Top Assister • 2011 Copa America Top Assister	

MESSI VERSUS RONALDO		
	MESSI	**RONALDO**
ALL COMPETITIONS		
APPEARANCES	1047	1204
ASSISTS	361	247
GOALS	821	873
Club		
APPEARANCES	867	999
ASSISTS	308	214
GOALS	715	745
CHAMPIONS LEAGUE		
APPEARANCES	163	183

ASSISTS	40	41
GOALS	129	140

Copa del Rey, Coppa Italia, FA Cup, EFL Cup, Coupe de France, Saudi King Cup, MLS Cup, US Open Cup		
APPEARANCES	83	83
ASSISTS	35	10
GOALS	56	46

All time Internationals		
APPEARANCES	180	205
ASSISTS	53	35
GOALS	106	128

THE GAME REINVENTED BY MESSI

Messi's exceptional ball-handling prowess is an undeniable force on the field, capturing the attention of every spectator. The way the ball adheres to his feet is nothing short of mesmerizing, as if his very being was designed to manipulate it flawlessly. His extraordinary control over the ball has the power to transform games, breathing new life into them with his astonishing manoeuvres. With every touch, he conjures an abundance of scoring opportunities, and it is nothing short of extraordinary that a staggering 90% of these chances culminate in goals, thanks to the final touch of the skilled individual who delivers the ball into the net.

Messi's passion on the field is unparalleled, but it is his unwavering determination to possess the ball and his unwavering confidence in his ball-handling skills that truly sets him apart. He has mastered the art of dribbling to such an extent that he is hailed as the ultimate dribble master by football analysts. His ability to effortlessly manoeuvre past defenders and create scoring opportunities is unmatched, making him the foremost player to be reckoned with when it comes to controlling the ball and orchestrating goals. Messi's exceptional skills and contributions to the game have cemented his status as the unrivalled best footballer in the world today and solidify his place among the all-time greats in the history of the sport. Messi's deep passion for football transcends words, as he holds an immense gratitude towards FC Barcelona for the profound impact it has had on his life and illustrious career thus far. Looking ahead, he eagerly envisions a continued alliance with the club, as his own heartfelt sentiments unequivocally affirm this unwavering commitment.

"Barcelona is not just a club to me, it is my entire existence. It has shaped me into the person I am today, and I am eternally grateful for that. The thought of leaving this beloved city and club is simply inconceivable to me. While I acknowledge the immense quality of the Premier League, I cannot fathom myself playing in England because my heart will forever belong to Barcelona. It is an unbreakable bond that will always guide my decisions.".

Lionel Messi's extraordinary talent knows no boundaries, captivating clubs both domestically and internationally. His mesmerizing style of play has left clubs worldwide in awe, igniting an intense desire to have him grace their teams. The fervour surrounding Messi's potential transfers has become a subject of amusement among fans, who delight in making playful remarks about the rumoured or actual offers he receives. In jest, they boldly declare, "Lionel Messi, name your price, for we are willing to surpass even your wildest expectations with our bid."

Messi's value to Barcelona FC is immeasurable, to the extent that his absence due to injury is the only scenario that could prevent his utilization on the field. The club and his teammates are fully aware of his extraordinary capabilities and recognize his indispensable role in securing victories in every match. Messi's greatness in football knows no limits, as evidenced by his astonishing records that trail behind him like an ever-present shadow. Consequently, the desire to emulate Messi's unparalleled skills and achievements is an overwhelming sentiment shared by all. The evidence from Messi's illustrious career beyond his domestic league with Barcelona FC undeniably supports the fervent aspirations of his devoted fans. Notably, Messi has proven himself to be an undisputed champion with his national team, Argentina. His remarkable achievements include clinching an Olympic Gold Medal, a testament to his exceptional skills and unwavering determination. Furthermore, Messi led his team to the grand finale of the prestigious World Cup last year, despite the unfortunate display of his Argentine strike partners, who unfortunately faltered in their attempts to find the back of the net. In stark contrast, Ronaldo, while not performing poorly for Portugal, has failed to reach the same extraordinary levels of excellence as Messi.

In the comprehensive analysis of Messi's exceptional ball-handling skills, it is crucial to highlight one of his most remarkable attributes: his unwavering determination to stay on his feet when faced with tackles on the field. Not only does he refuse to succumb easily to challenges, but he also refrains from engaging in any form of simulation or play-acting. Messi's integrity is truly commendable, as he rarely resorts to diving to deceive referees and gain unfair advantages. This sets him apart from his counterpart Ronaldo, who unfortunately carries a tarnished reputation for frequently diving. Despite facing disciplinary actions for simulation in the past, Ronaldo often manages to evade penalties for his dive-induced theatrics, a practice he had even employed during his time at Manchester United.

MESSI, BEST PLAYER OF ALL TIMES

Lionel Messi, the football maestro, faced relentless criticism during his struggles with Argentina. Detractors claimed, "He only shines with Barcelona," "He fails to deliver in crucial matches for Argentina," and "He relies on the brilliance of Xavi and Iniesta to succeed." These derogatory remarks aimed to undermine Messi's remarkable feats, preventing him from being hailed as the greatest player of all time. However, there was one missing accolade that could silence the naysayers and solidify his legacy – a triumphant title at the international level.

When Lionel Messi achieved the remarkable feat of leading Argentina to victory in the Copa America last year, it seemed as though he had reached the pinnacle of his career. However, the goalposts of greatness were once again shifted, as he faced the daunting task of winning the World Cup to solidify his claim as the greatest of all time. Astonishingly, Messi has now achieved that monumental feat as well, guiding Argentina to a glorious triumph over France in a thrilling penalty shootout.

For over a decade, the debate surrounding the best footballer in the world has revolved around Messi and Cristiano Ronaldo. However, with Messi's triumphant World Cup victory, that debate has been unequivocally silenced. The question of whether Messi deserves the title of the greatest of all time has also been definitively answered. The answer is resoundingly clear: Yes, Lionel Messi is undeniably the greatest men's soccer player in the history of the sport.

Messi's exceptional skills, unrivaled talent, and countless achievements have solidified his place at the pinnacle of soccer greatness. His ability to mesmerize with his sublime dribbling, astound with his pinpoint accuracy, and inspire with his unmatched vision on the field is unparalleled. Messi's record-breaking goal-scoring prowess and numerous individual accolades further cement his status as a true legend of the game.

Beyond his individual brilliance, Messi's impact on his team and country cannot be overstated. His leadership, determination, and unwavering commitment have propelled Argentina to unprecedented success on the global stage. Messi's ability to inspire and elevate the performance of his teammates is a testament to his exceptional character and unwavering desire to win.

In conclusion, there is no longer any room for doubt or debate. Lionel Messi's awe-inspiring achievements, coupled with his unmatched skill and unwavering dedication, have firmly established him as the greatest men's soccer player of all time. His name will forever be etched in the annals of football history, serving as an enduring testament to his unparalleled greatness.

Lionel Messi: Personal Accolades	
YEAR	**ACCOLADE**
2008	Summer Olympics: Gold medal
2004/2005	FIFA World Youth Championship
2012/2013	Golden Boot
2012/2013	League Top Scorer
2012	FIFA Ballon d'Or
2011/2012	Golden Boot
2011/2012	Champions League Top Scorer
2011/2012	League Top Scorer
2011	FIFA Ballon d'Or
2010/2011	Champions League Top Scorer
2010	FIFA Ballon d'Or

Lionel Messi: Personal Accolades	
YEAR	ACCOLADE
2009/2010	Golden Boot
2009/2010	Champions League Top Scorer
2009/2010	League Top Scorer
2009	FIFA World Player
2009	FIFA Ballon d'Or
2008/2009	Champions League Top Scorer
2008	2nd alternative FIFA WORLD PLAYER
2007	2nd alternative FIFA WORLD PLAYER.

The table below presents Messi's major honours.

Lionel Messi: Major Honors	
FOOTBALL CLUB / COUNTRY HONOR	YEAR
Barcelona	
Spanish La Liga Title(*6):	2004-2005, 2005-06, 2008-2009, 2009-2010, 2010-11, 2012-2013
Spanish Cup (*2)—Copa del Rey:	2008-2009, 2011-2012
Spanish Cup Runner-up	2010-11
Super Copa de España (*6):	2005, 2006, 2009, 2010, 2011, 2013
Super Copa de España Runner-Up:	2012
UEFA Champions League (*3) :	2005-2006, 2008-2009, 2010-2011
UEFA Super Cup Runner Up:	2006
UEFA Super Cup (*2):	2009, 2011
FIFA Club World Cup (2):	2009, 2011
Argentina	
Olympic Gold Medal:	2008
FIFA U-20 World Cup:	2005
World Cup—Quarter-Final	2006
World Cup—Quarter-Final	2010

Lionel Messi: Major Honors	
FOOTBALL CLUB / COUNTRY HONOR	**YEAR**
World Cup—Runner Up	2014
World Cup--Winner	2022

Given the multitude of accolades and achievements that Lionel Messi has garnered throughout his illustrious career, there is an undeniable truth that resonates - he stands unrivalled as the greatest player to have ever graced the world of football. With a mesmerizing display of skill, finesse, and unparalleled consistency, Messi's dominance on the field is unparalleled, leaving no room for debate or dispute. It is an unequivocal fact that no other individual, past, or present, possesses the sheer talent, versatility, and impact that Lionel Messi embodies, solidifying his status as the epitome of footballing excellence.

THE 2022 WORLD CUP RECITAL

The highly anticipated and monumental event that will captivate the entire globe, the grandiose recital of the illustrious 2022 World Cup final, will undoubtedly be etched in the annals of history. With the world's finest football talents converging on the hallowed grounds of the stadium, the atmosphere will be electrifying, charged with an unparalleled intensity that only such a prestigious occasion can generate.

As the roaring crowd fills the colossal arena, their voices blending harmoniously to create a symphony of anticipation, the air crackles with an almost tangible energy. The mesmerizing display of skill, strategy, and sheer determination exhibited by the world-class athletes will leave spectators breathless, their hearts pounding in sync with each exhilarating moment.

The deafening cheers and thunderous applause will reverberate through the stadium, as fans from every corner of the globe unite in their unwavering support for their respective teams. Flags waving proudly, painted faces, and jerseys adorned with the colors of their nations, the passionate supporters will create a kaleidoscope of fervor, transforming the stadium into a vibrant tapestry of unity.

The players, adorned in their iconic national kits, will take to the field with a fire in their eyes, their hearts pulsating with the weight of their country's hopes and dreams. Every pass, every shot, and every tackle will be executed with precision and finesse, as the battle for football supremacy reaches its zenith.

The tension will mount as the match progresses, with each team relentlessly vying for the coveted title of World Cup champions. The tactical masterminds on the sidelines will orchestrate their strategies, making calculated substitutions and adjustments, leaving no stone unturned in their pursuit of victory.

As the final whistle looms, the intensity will reach its climax, with both teams summoning every ounce of their strength, skill, and determination. The world will hold its breath, collectively suspended in a moment of anticipation, as the fate of the match hangs in the balance.

Finally, amidst a crescendo of emotions, the victor will emerge, basking in the glory of triumph, while the vanquished will leave the field with heads held high, knowing they gave their all in pursuit of greatness. The jubilant celebrations and tearful embraces will encapsulate the essence of the World Cup, a testament to the unifying power of sport and the indomitable spirit of humanity.

The recital of the 2022 World Cup final will transcend the boundaries of a mere sporting event, etching itself into the collective memory of generations to come. It will stand as a testament to the pinnacle of athletic prowess, the culmination of years of dedication and sacrifice, and the enduring legacy of the beautiful game.

The statistics spoke for themselves, leaving no room for doubt. History had shown that losing the first game in group play greatly diminished the chances of progressing to the knockout round. However, Argentina defied the odds, not only advancing but emerging as the group winner, and their victorious streak remained unbroken. In a thrilling match against the reigning champions, France, Argentina secured a remarkable 3-3 draw, ultimately triumphing with a 4-2 penalty kick shootout victory. This monumental achievement now allows Lionel Messi, the football legend, to proudly claim the title of a World Cup champion, possibly in his last ever World Cup appearance. Argentina's remarkable feat marks their third World Cup triumph, causing the initial murmurs of doubt to be replaced by tears of joy and resounding cheers of celebration.

Argentina entered the match against France with an unwavering determination and an unyielding barrage of attacks. Despite France's previous displays of dominance throughout the tournament, they found themselves grappling to regain their rhythm, cohesion, and the electrifying energy they had exhibited in Qatar.

The Argentina attack proved to be incredibly fruitful as they relentlessly pressed forward, resulting in a pivotal breakthrough during the first half. Displaying his exceptional agility and skill, Argentina's forward, Ángel Di María, swiftly maneuverer past France's Ousmane Dembélé, who unfortunately resorted to tripping him inside the penalty box. This skilful play by Di María not only earned Argentina a penalty kick but also highlighted his ability to outmanoeuvre and outwit his opponents.

Lionel Messi, the undisputed maestro of the game, stood tall on the grandest stage of them all, his 26th appearance in the World Cup, a record unmatched by any other player in the history of the men's tournament. As he approached the penalty spot, the atmosphere crackled with anticipation, for there was no doubt that he was destined to seize this moment. With unwavering composure, he took a deep breath, channelling his immense focus and skill. The ball left his foot with an elegant precision, gliding low and true towards the right corner of the net, leaving the French goalkeeper rooted to the spot. The stadium erupted in a symphony of euphoria as the scoreboard displayed a resounding 1-0 in favour of Messi's team.

In a remarkable feat, Lionel Messi etched his name in history by becoming the first player ever to find the back of the net in every single game of a World Cup knockout round within a solitary tournament. From the intense round of 16 clashes to the high-stakes quarterfinals, nerve-wracking semifinals, and the grand finale itself, Messi's unwavering goal-scoring prowess remained unmatched. This unprecedented achievement solidifies his status as a true legend of the game, forever etching his name in the annals of football history.

The South American team displayed relentless determination as they refused to back down. In the 36th minute, Argentina showcased their exceptional skill by flawlessly breaking through the French defense right from the midfield. With remarkable precision, Di María emerged as the architect of opportunities once again, swiftly advancing towards the goal and expertly lifting a shot that soared gracefully above the outstretched arms of the diving French goalkeeper, Hugo Lloris. This incredible play resulted in Argentina securing a 2-0 lead, leaving the spectators in awe of their exceptional performance.

Overwhelmed with emotion, Di María, the passionate Argentinean player, trotted back to his homeland's side of the field, tears streaming down his face, as the deafening roar of the crowd echoed in his ears.

France appeared completely disoriented and disjointed on the field, clearly struggling to find their rhythm. In a surprising move, Coach Didier Deschamps made a bold and unprecedented decision by substituting not just one, but two of his key players during the first half. The first casualty was Dembélé, whose unfortunate foul resulted in the opposing team's opening goal. Additionally, Deschamps shockingly replaced Olivier Giroud, the all-time leading scorer for the French national team. This audacious decision by the coach sent shockwaves throughout the stadium, leaving fans and pundits alike questioning his strategy and the future of the team's performance.

At the halfway mark, the reigning champions, France, were left utterly astounded by the turn of events unfolding on the pitch. The highly acclaimed French prodigy, Kylian Mbappé, failed to exhibit his usual brilliance throughout the initial 45 minutes of the fierce encounter.

Mbappé's brilliance illuminated the entirety of the 2018 World Cup, captivating the world's attention at the tender age of 19. His extraordinary performances drew countless comparisons to the legendary Pelé, another prodigious teenager who had left an indelible mark on the soccer world. In a remarkable feat, Mbappé became the first teenager since Pelé in 1958 to grace a World Cup final with his goal-scoring prowess. Fast forward to the 2022 tournament, and Mbappé seamlessly continued his awe-inspiring journey, showcasing his exceptional skills and reaffirming his status as a true footballing phenomenon.

In a truly remarkable feat, he not only broke Pelé's long-standing record for a player under 24 by scoring an astonishing 12 goals in the World Cup, but also emerged as a fierce contender for the overall goal lead, tying with the legendary Messi. However, even against formidable opponents like Argentina, Mbappé's exceptional performance was somewhat stifled, as he was left with minimal opportunities to showcase his prowess. It wasn't until the 71st minute that he finally unleashed his first recorded shot, a testament to the remarkable defensive efforts against him.

The atmosphere inside Lusail Stadium was nothing short of electrifying as the tremendous crowd of nearly 89,000 passionate individuals overwhelmingly rallied behind Argentina, proudly donning the team's iconic white and sky blue uniform. Their unwavering support echoed throughout the stadium, as they erupted into thunderous cheers for every single touch, every precise pass, and every daring shot taken by their beloved team.

However, in a thrilling turn of events during the 80th minute, Mbappé dramatically narrowed the Argentina lead by successfully converting a penalty shot, reducing the scoreline to 2-1. Throughout the entire match, France had been subdued, lacking confidence, and displaying a sense of uncertainty. Yet, in that pivotal moment, the dynamics of the game shifted dramatically as France suddenly ignited with Vigor and determination.

In a stunning turn of events, a mere 93 seconds later, the incredible Mbappé once again left spectators in awe. With sheer determination, he unleashed a scorching right-footed strike that surpassed the grasp of the formidable Argentinian goalkeeper, Emiliano Martínez. The scoreboard now read 2-2, as Mbappé single-handedly restored equilibrium to the game.

This is the highly anticipated French team that spectators have been eagerly awaiting to witness in the championship. The long-awaited clash between the legendary 35-year-old Messi, widely regarded as one of the greatest players in history, and the exceptional 23-year-old Mbappé, who consistently enhances his already remarkable soccer career, has finally arrived.

The intense match between the teams extended beyond the regular 90 minutes, as they battled it out for an additional nine minutes in regulation time and an intense eight minutes in stoppage time. Despite their relentless efforts, neither team managed to find the back of the net, resulting in an exhilarating 30 minutes of extra time being enforced.

Argentina, despite their previous experience, found themselves in a hauntingly familiar situation once again. In a cruel twist of fate, history repeated itself as they suffered defeat in the 2014 World Cup final, reminiscent of their heart-wrenching loss to Germany. The match was a fierce battle that pushed both teams to their limits, but ultimately Argentina was left shattered when Germany managed to break the deadlock in extra time, securing a devastating 1-0 victory.

In a thrilling turn of events during extra time, it was Argentina who emerged victorious by finding the back of the net. Unsurprisingly, the one to deliver this crucial blow was none other than the legendary Lionel Messi. With the ball bouncing wildly in front of the French goal, Messi's unwavering determination led him to powerfully boot it past the goalkeeper. This remarkable feat occurred in the 109th minute, marking Messi's second goal of the evening and solidifying Argentina's lead with a score of 3-2.

Naturally, it was expected that the current score would not remain unchanged for long. As fate would have it, a handling violation occurred within the Argentine box, subsequently granting France yet another opportunity for a penalty kick. And as if by some predetermined script, the renowned Mbappé was the chosen one to take the shot. Unsurprisingly, he flawlessly converted it into a remarkable goal during the intense 118th minute. Thus, the young French prodigy achieved an extraordinary hat trick, solidifying his status as a rising star. The scoreboard now displayed an exhilarating 3-3 tie, leaving spectators in awe of the remarkable turn of events.

In an exhilarating display of skill and determination, both teams fiercely clashed in the dying minutes of the match, leaving spectators on the edge of their seats. However, the fate of this monumental World Cup final was ultimately decided by an electrifying penalty kick shootout, destined to be forever etched in the annals of football history as the most awe-inspiring and unforgettable showdown ever witnessed.

Argentina gained an early advantage in the match, showcasing their prowess. As the tension escalated, both Kylian Mbappé and Lionel Messi successfully converted their penalty kicks, adding fuel to the already intense atmosphere. However, the Argentina goalkeeper exhibited exceptional skill and denied France's Kingsley Coman from finding the back of the net. The stakes were high as Aurélien Tchouaméni stepped up to take his shot, but unfortunately, he failed to capitalize on the opportunity. Ultimately, it all boiled down to Gonzalo Montiel, who displayed nerves of steel and confidently scored the decisive penalty kick, securing a triumphant victory for Argentina. The scene that followed was filled with a plethora of emotions - tears of joy, heartfelt hugs, and radiant smiles adorned the faces of both Messi and the entire Argentine team, truly exemplifying their collective elation.

Argentina's triumphant victory in the World Cup dates back to 1986, an unforgettable moment when Diego Maradona led the team to glory. Since then, the nation has yearned for another taste of that unparalleled success. Maradona, a legendary figure whose influence and legacy have cast an immense shadow, has become an indomitable presence in Lionel Messi's journey towards greatness. The weight of Maradona's legacy looms large over Messi, serving as a constant reminder of the immense challenge and responsibility that comes with carrying the hopes and dreams of a nation on his shoulders.

In an unprecedented triumph, the highly anticipated 2022 World Cup unequivocally belongs to the football powerhouse, Argentina. This monumental victory not only marks Argentina's remarkable third title in the history of the tournament but also signifies a momentous milestone for the legendary Lionel Messi. After years of relentless dedication and unwavering commitment to the sport, Messi can finally revel in the glory of being crowned a World Cup champion for the very first time. This resounding achievement not only solidifies his status as one of the greatest footballers of all time but also serves as a testament to his unwavering perseverance and indomitable spirit. With this historic win, Messi's illustrious career reaches its pinnacle, leaving his remarkable resume adorned with every accolade imaginable.

INSIGHTFUL QUOTES FROM LIONEL MESSI

Messi's personal quotes transcend the realm of ordinary player statements, etching themselves into the annals of football history as indelible and remarkable. Delving into his profound insights about his personal life and on-field performance, one cannot help but be astounded by his unwavering analytical prowess, unfiltered honesty, unwavering directness, and unparalleled passion for his craft. These profound glimpses into Messi's psyche provide a profound understanding of the man behind the footballer, unravelling the layers that define his character and illuminating the essence of his unparalleled skills.

"I have always believed that talent alone is not enough to achieve greatness. It is the combination of hard work, dedication, and a relentless passion for the game that truly sets one apart. Football is not just a sport to me; it is a way of life, an expression of my innermost emotions and desires. With every touch of the ball, I strive to create magic, to inspire others, and to leave a legacy. The road to success is never easy, but it is the challenges and obstacles that fuel my determination to push beyond my limits. I am grateful for every setback, for they have taught me invaluable lessons and made me stronger. My personal mantra is simple yet profound: Dream big, work harder, and never stop believing in yourself. For it is through perseverance and unwavering faith that dreams are transformed into reality."

"CHAMPIONS OF THE WORLD!!!!!!!" Messi ecstatically exclaimed in his native Spanish on the social media post. Overwhelmed with emotions, he confessed, "I have dreamt of this moment countless times, yearned for it so intensely that I still can't wrap my mind around it... I am in disbelief." Overflowing with gratitude, he expressed heartfelt appreciation to his family, all his unwavering supporters, and those who had faith in the team. Once again, Argentina has demonstrated their indomitable spirit, proving that when we unite and fight together, we can conquer any obstacle. The credit belongs to this remarkable group, transcending individual efforts, as it is the collective strength that propelled us towards this shared dream, a dream that resonates with every Argentine. We have done it!!! LET'S GO ARGENTINA DAMN!!!!! We will reunite very soon."

"I had envisioned it, I yearned for it with all my heart": Messi's Instagram post radiating joy and fulfilment after triumphing in the FIFA World Cup.

"Each passing year, I relentlessly strive to transcend my limitations as a player and avoid falling into the stagnation of routine. My unwavering commitment lies in incessantly refining every facet of my game, leaving no stone unturned in the pursuit of improvement".

"Monetary gain does not serve as a driving force for me. Its allure fails to ignite any additional passion or enhance my performance, as the perks of wealth hold little significance. My true contentment lies solely in the presence of a ball at my feet. The game I adore is the wellspring of my motivation. Even if I were not compensated for my skills as a professional footballer, I would willingly partake in the sport without any monetary reward."

"At the onset of each year, our primary goal is to emerge victorious as a cohesive team, leaving no stone unturned in our pursuit of glory. While personal achievements hold value, they take a backseat to the collective triumph we strive to achieve together."

"I dedicate myself to rising early and working diligently until late hours, consistently persevering day after day, year after year. It is through this unwavering commitment that I have achieved what many perceive as an overnight success, although the reality is that it took me precisely 17 years and 114 days to reach this pinnacle of accomplishment."

"You possess the incredible power to conquer any obstacle that comes your way, as long as you wholeheartedly embrace a deep and unwavering love for something or someone."

"Success is not handed to you on a silver platter; it demands an unwavering determination to overcome obstacles and pursue your dreams relentlessly. It requires making sacrifices and dedicating yourself to a tireless work ethic. Only through this relentless pursuit can you transform your aspirations into reality."

"I may be known for my extraordinary talents, but at the core, I am just an ordinary individual leading a remarkably relatable life. Beyond the spotlight and the accolades, once I'm done showcasing my skills and fulfilling my professional duties, I immerse myself in the embrace of my cherished family, loyal friends, and experience the joys and challenges of everyday existence, just like any other individual."

"I have harboured an unwavering aspiration to become a World Champion, and I refused to relinquish my pursuit, even in the face of the daunting possibility that it may forever elude me."

"Regardless of the nature of the game, be it a friendly match, a competitive fixture, a high-stakes final, or any other encounter, my approach remains unwavering. I consistently strive to embody excellence, not only for the benefit of my team and my own personal growth, but also to gratify the ardent supporters who rally behind us. My ultimate objective is to seize victory and leave an indelible mark on the field."

"I approach every game with a relentless determination, pouring my heart and soul into giving my absolute best. I refuse to let the thought of potential fouls from opponents, or the fear of injury consume my mind. I firmly believe that dwelling on such concerns only serves to hinder your performance and growth."

"In life, it is crucial to acknowledge the reality that achieving victory in every endeavour is simply unattainable. Embracing this truth becomes an essential step towards personal growth and resilience."

Based on the quotes provided, it is evident that Messi's contributions to the team have remained consistent since his early days at Barcelona. As a young boy, he dedicated himself to the team's improvement, displaying unwavering commitment. Money is not the driving force behind Messi's motivation. While it is natural for most people to appreciate financial gain, for Messi, it plays a negligible role in his passion for the sport. His true joy lies solely on the field, and it is likely that he would continue playing even without any monetary compensation. Football runs through his veins, and his love for the game is not dictated by his wallet. The feeling is mutual, as football also holds a deep affection for Messi.

"There is an indescribable sense of magnificence and splendour that accompanies being recognized as one of the finest in any endeavour. However, without the acquisition of titles and victories, all accomplishments seem to lose their significance and allure."

"Every passing day, I am steadily improving my skills and abilities. My unwavering dedication to playing remains intact, as I am fuelled by an undying passion to excel in my craft."

From a young age, my passion for football consumed me, captivating my every waking moment. While my peers sought out social gatherings and adventures, I willingly sacrificed those fleeting pleasures to nurture my dedication to the sport. Countless occasions arose where my friends beckoned me to join their escapades, yet I steadfastly declined, opting instead to remain within the confines of my home, knowing that the following day held a crucial practice session.

It is abundantly clear that Messi is not only grateful but also deeply committed to FC Barcelona. The owners, coaches, and fellow players have fostered a strong sense of belonging and dependency within him, making it highly unlikely for him to ever consider leaving. Even if the day were to come when

Messi departs, it would not be of his own volition, but rather a decision made by the team itself. This decision could stem from the belief that his salary no longer aligns with the level of his performance, or perhaps to support him in the final phase of his illustrious career. Unlike many other players who succumb to the insatiable desire for wealth and opt to play for the highest bidder, Messi should be hailed as an exemplar of loyalty, someone who has stood by his team through thick and thin. He has consistently rejected lucrative offers from other clubs, which would have doubled his already impressive Barcelona salary.

"I have grown accustomed to the bustling atmosphere of photoshoots and videos, where a multitude of people gather, along with the electrifying energy of football. Witnessing the meticulous preparation that goes into these events has become an integral part of my everyday existence. It is truly gratifying to observe the sheer dedication and readiness of the entire team, all working harmoniously towards a common goal. Do I relish this experience? Absolutely! It encapsulates the essence of life itself, leaving no room for any alternative."

"There is truly no greater source of fulfilment than witnessing the sheer joy and radiance of a contented, beaming child. I wholeheartedly dedicate myself to helping in any capacity possible, whether it be a simple act of endorsing my signature on an autograph. Undoubtedly, the priceless value of a child's genuine smile surpasses any material wealth that exists in this world."

In this powerful statement, Lionel Messi reveals his deep desire to make a positive impact on the lives of others. Not only is he an exceptional football player, but he also dedicates his time and resources to philanthropic endeavors. One of his notable contributions is his involvement with the United Nations Children's Fund (UNICEF), an organization that Barcelona FC also supports strongly.

Recognizing Messi's commitment to making a difference, UNICEF appointed him as a Goodwill Ambassador in March 2010. Just four months later, he embarked on his first field mission to Haiti, a country devastated by an earthquake, to shed light on the dire situation of its children. By using his platform and influence, Messi brought public awareness to the challenges they faced and the urgent need for assistance.

Moreover, Messi actively participates in UNICEF campaigns that address critical issues such as HIV prevention, education, and the social inclusion of disabled children. His involvement goes beyond financial contributions, as he actively engages in raising awareness and advocating for these causes. This demonstrates his genuine dedication to improving the lives of vulnerable children around the world.

In November 2013, Messi celebrated his first son's birthday in a remarkable way. Alongside his son Thiago, he joined a publicity campaign aimed at raising awareness about the alarming mortality rates among disadvantaged children. By lending his voice and support to this cause, Messi showcased his compassion and determination to make a difference in the lives of those who are less fortunate.

Through his philanthropic efforts, Messi exemplifies the true essence of a role model and a compassionate human being. His unwavering commitment to helping others, as demonstrated through his work with UNICEF and other initiatives, sets an inspiring example for individuals across the globe.

In a remarkable display of compassion and dedication to making a positive impact on the lives of children, Lionel Messi, the renowned footballer, and UNICEF ambassador, has gone above and beyond by establishing his own charitable organization, the Lionel Messi Foundation. This incredible foundation focuses on providing crucial support in the areas of healthcare, education, and sports for children in need.

The genesis of this inspiring foundation can be traced back to Messi's visit to the Massachusetts General Hospital for Children in Boston, where he witnessed firsthand the incredible work being done to care for children battling terminal illnesses. The profound impact of this experience resonated deeply with

Messi, prompting him to act and utilize a portion of his earnings to give back to society.

Through the Lionel Messi Foundation, Messi has been able to make a substantial difference in the lives of countless children. By awarding research grants, financing medical training programs, and investing in the development of medical centers and projects, Messi has demonstrated his unwavering commitment to improving the healthcare landscape for children not only in his home country of Argentina but also in Spain and various other nations.

It is truly awe-inspiring to witness the extent of Messi's dedication to creating a better future for children in need. By leveraging his platform and resources, he has become a beacon of hope, shining a light on the importance of access to quality healthcare, education, and sports for all children. Messi's philanthropic efforts serve as a powerful reminder that even the smallest acts of kindness can have an immeasurable impact on the lives of those who need it the most.

.

WORLD QUOTES ABOUT MESSI

LIONEL MESSI'S STATS
World Cup 2022

		Rank
Goals	7	2nd
Shots	32	1st
Assists	3	1st
Chances created	21	2nd
Dribbles completed	15	3rd

These heartfelt words were expressed by none other than Leo Messi himself, reflecting on his incredible journey from his humble beginnings in Grandoli to the grand stage of the World Cup in Qatar. Almost three decades have passed since he first started playing with the ball, a period filled with countless moments of joy and occasional sorrow. Throughout it all, Messi held onto his dream of becoming a World Champion, never allowing himself to give up, even when the odds seemed against him.

In his message, Messi acknowledges that the victory in this World Cup belongs not only to him and his teammates, but also to those who came before them. He pays tribute to the previous World Cups, particularly the 2014 tournament in Brazil, where the team fought valiantly until the very end, deserving a win that eluded them. Messi also dedicates this triumph to the late

Diego Maradona, who watched over them from above, providing unwavering support and inspiration.

Furthermore, Messi recognizes the unwavering support of the fans and all those who have stood by the National Team, regardless of the outcome. Their belief and passion have been a driving force throughout the years, even during the moments when things didn't go according to plan.

Lastly, Messi extends his gratitude to the entire national team, including the coaching staff and the anonymous individuals who work tirelessly behind the scenes. Their dedication and hard work have played a crucial role in ensuring that the team can perform at their best, day in and day out.

In these words, Messi not only celebrates his personal triumph but also acknowledges the collective effort and sacrifices that have led to this moment of glory. It is a testament to his humility, gratitude, and the profound impact that this victory holds for him and the entire nation.

"These powerful words are spoken by none other than the legendary Leo Messi himself, who marvels at the captivating narrative that football weaves, forever enthralling us with its magic. In a world where dreams come true, Messi's long-awaited triumph in winning his first World Cup shines as a testament to his extraordinary journey. It is an awe-inspiring spectacle that leaves us in awe, witnessing the glorious future of our beloved sport unfold before our very eyes. With heartfelt congratulations to Argentina, Messi acknowledges that the late Diego Maradona, an icon of the game, must be looking down upon them with a radiant smile."

"These are the resounding words of the legendary Leo Messi, echoing the sentiments of an entire nation: "ALBERTO FERNANDEZ, the esteemed Argentine President, let us forever stand united, bound by an unbreakable bond. WE HAVE TRIUMPHED, emerging as the undeniable champions of the world. In this moment of sheer euphoria, words fail to capture the magnitude of our achievement. With utmost gratitude, we extend our heartfelt THANK YOU."

These awe-inspiring words were spoken by none other than the legendary Leo Messi himself, as he paid tribute to the remarkable achievements of Roger Federer, a true titan of tennis with an astounding 20 Grand Slam titles under his belt. Messi, in awe of Federer's unparalleled success, hailed it as nothing short of a fairytale come true for Argentina. Messi further acknowledged that time and time again, Federer has not only epitomized greatness but has also continuously pushed the boundaries of what is possible in his sport. Messi considered it an absolute honour and privilege to bear witness to Federer's remarkable journey of triumph and excellence.

These powerful words come from none other than the legendary Leo Messi himself, who holds no reservations in proclaiming Andy Murray, the three-time Grand Slam champion, as an exceptional athlete. Messi's admiration extends beyond the realm of football, recognizing Murray's unparalleled achievements and character. Such high praise from a sporting icon like Messi only solidifies Murray's status as an extraordinary individual who has left an indelible mark on the world of sports.

"Let me extend my heartfelt congratulations to Argentina for achieving this incredible victory in honour of Messi! Their remarkable comeback from the initial stages of the campaign is truly commendable."

Tiger Woods, a legendary 15-time major champion in golf, expressed his awe and admiration for Lionel Messi, hailing him as the greatest soccer player he has ever witnessed. While acknowledging the greatness of football icons like Pele and Maradona, Woods emphasized that Messi's unparalleled ball control, where the ball seems to be glued to his foot, leaves him astounded. The level of skill and finesse displayed by Messi is simply mind-boggling, solidifying his status as an exceptional talent in the world of soccer.

"Lionel Scaloni, in awe, expressed his astonishment at the incomparable influence Lionel Messi has on his team-mates. He emphasized that Messi's ability to transmit unmatched energy and inspiration is a phenomenon he has never witnessed before. Not only is Messi an exceptional player, but he also selflessly dedicates himself to uplifting and empowering his team-mates, making him an invaluable asset."

Sid Lowe expressed his awe and admiration by questioning how one can truly capture the greatness of this individual. The abundance of superlatives has long been exhausted, leaving us grasping for ways to adequately convey their extraordinary talent. Even resorting to profanity or attempting to symbolize the indescribable seems futile at this point.

Pep Guardiola, the esteemed football manager, expressed his awe-inspiring admiration for Lionel Messi, stating that attempting to capture the essence of the legendary player in words would be futile. Guardiola urged everyone to abandon the futile task of describing Messi's brilliance and instead advised them to simply witness his extraordinary talent unfold on the field.

CONCLUSION

The development of Lionel Messi's professional character is a topic that has been extensively discussed, but it is crucial to focus on the characteristics that truly define him as a player and his remarkable contributions to the sport. What sets Messi apart is not just his talent, but also the incredible fame he has attained beyond his physical stature. One would expect his height to be a hindrance to his game, but it has proven to be a hidden advantage. Messi's personality is captivating, and many aspire to emulate him, both now and in the future. Youngsters worldwide look up to him as a role model in football, not only because of his outstanding skills, but also because of his unwavering passion for the game. Despite facing medical challenges, Messi continues to excel and assumes the role of the "best" in football. When evaluating his achievements and comparing him to other players of his time, it is evident that Messi's accomplishments are unparalleled. His extraordinary success is likely to continue to surpass all expectations.

After countless dreams and an insatiable desire, Lionel Messi, Argentina's legendary forward, has finally achieved the unimaginable. The long-awaited and highly coveted FIFA World Cup trophy now graces his illustrious hall of fame. In a captivating showdown against France, on the momentous day of 18th December 2022 in Qatar, Argentina emerged victorious, putting an end to a month-long carnival of football brilliance. This triumph solidifies Messi's status as one of the greatest footballers of all time, etching his name in the annals of sporting history.

Signature

Leo MESSI Signature

REFERENCES

1. "Lionel Messi: The Greatest Player in History" by Jean Bercy (the book itself)

2. "Messi: The Inside Story of the Boy Who Became a Legend" by Luca Caioli

3. "Messi: A Biography" by Leonardo Faccio

4. "Lionel Messi: The Ultimate Fan Book" by Iain Spragg

5. "Messi: The Children's Illustration Book" by Michael Part

6. "Lionel Messi: The Flea - The Amazing Story of Leo Messi" by Michael Part

7. "Lionel Messi: The Ultimate Superstar" by Alain Louyot

8. "Messi: The Rise of a Legend" by Guillem Balague

9. "Lionel Messi: The Inspirational Story of Soccer's Greatest Superstar" by Bill Redban

10. "Lionel Messi: The Ultimate Fan Guide" by Adrian Besley

11. "Lionel Messi: Above all" by Jean Bercy

Made in the USA
Columbia, SC
19 March 2025